ON THE ORIGIN

OF THE

INDIAN BRAHMA ALPHABET

ON THE ORIGIN

OF THE

INDIAN BRAHMA ALPHABET.

GEORG BUHLER

GYAN

Published by

Gyan Publishing House
5, Ansari Road
Daryaganj, New Delhi-110002
Phone: 011-47034999, 9811692060
E-mail: books@gyanbooks.com

Distribution Network
gyanbooks.com
India, USA, Canada, UK, Australia, France

ISBN : 978-81-212-9526-0 (PB)
First Published, 1898

2nd Impression 2023

Printed at: Gyan Press, Delhi.

ON THE ORIGIN OF THE INDIAN BRAHMA ALPHABET
Author: GEORG BUHLER

ON THE ORIGIN

OF THE

INDIAN BRĀHMA ALPHABET.

BY

GEORG BÜHLER.

SECOND REVISED EDITION OF INDIAN STUDIES, № III.

TOGETHER WITH TWO APPENDICES ON THE ORIGIN
OF THE KHAROṢṬHĪ ALPHABET AND OF THE
SO-CALLED LETTER-NUMERALS OF THE BRĀHMĪ.

1898.

Preface to the Second Edition.

As the few separate copies of the Indian Studies No. III, struck off in 1895, were sold very soon and rather numerous requests for additional ones were addressed both to me and to the bookseller of the Imperial Academy, Messrs. Carl Gerold's Sohn, I asked the Academy for permission to issue a second edition, which Mr. Karl J. Trübner had consented to publish. My petition was readily granted. In addition Messrs. von Hölder, the publishers of the Wiener Zeitschrift für die Kunde des Morgenlandes, kindly allowed me to reprint my article on the origin of the Kharoṣṭhī, which had appeared in vol. IX of that Journal and is now given in Appendix I. To these two sections I have added, in Appendix II, a brief review of the arguments for Dr. Burnell's hypothesis, which derives the so-called letter-numerals or numerical symbols of the Brāhma alphabet from the ancient Egyptian numeral signs, together with a third comparative table, in order to include in this volume all those points, which require fuller discussion, and in order to make it a serviceable companion to the palaeography of the Grundriss. The chapters on the Brāhmī and the Kharoṣṭhī have been throughout revised and the first has been changed most. A new comparative table of the Semitic and Brāhma signs,[1] the same as has been used for the Grundriss, has been given. The Additional Note at the end has been omitted, as, since the

[1] In using the plates, those of the Grundriss ought always to be compared, as the signs given there are mechanical reproductions from impressions and as such more reliable than any drawn by hand.

appearance of M. Sylvain Lévi's article[1] on the Turkish kingdom of Northwestern India, it is no longer required, and a number of other alterations and additions has been made in accordance with the results of further researches.

Thus the list of the passages from the Jātakas, which mention writing and written documents, has been considerably enlarged, the enlargement having become possible chiefly through references, kindly communicated to me by Professors S. von Oldenburg (p. 7 ff.) and Rhys Davids (p. 120).[2]

The extensive and intimate acquaintance of Lieut. Col. R. C. Temple with the actualities of daily Indian life has enabled me to adduce an interesting confirmation of my explanation of the term *rūpa* which occurs in the oldest known Indian *trivium* (p. 14, note 3).

A valuable paper by Dr. von Rosthorn, based on Chinese sources, has furnished a correction of the interpretation which I formerly put on Hiuen Tsiang's statement that in the seventh century A. D. the instruction of the young Hindus began with the twelve *chang* (p. 30). It now appears that the twelve *chang* were twelve tables of simple and compound letters, of which the *varṇamālā* or *mātṛkāviveka* of the period consisted. And a

---

[1] See Journ. Asiatique, 1895, série IX, t. VI, p. 380 f. I accept M. Lévi's conclusion that Major Deane's undeciphered inscriptions from Swāt are Turkish as highly probable, and I may add that a key prepared from the signs of Sanskrit and Prakrit inscriptions does not fit them.

[2] I regret that vol. VI of Professor Fausböll's edition of the Jātakas reached me too late for utilisation. It furnishes a number of additional passages, proving the use of writing, among which that on p. 369 f. is the most interesting. According to the story told there, Amarādevī, the daughter of the Sheth of Yavamajjhaka, noted on a leaf *(paṇṇa)*, when and by whom king Vedeha's crest-jewel, golden garland, golden slippers and precious rug were sent to her husband, Mahosadha. Afterwards she produced the record before the king to the confusion of his four Pandits, who had accused her husband of the theft of the articles, and whom she had captured and confined in baskets when they came to seduce her. As Prof. Minayeff has first seen, the scene in the king's court is illustrated by the Bharahut relievo, inscribed *yavamajhakiyaṃ jātakaṃ*, Cunningham, Bharhut Stûpa, pl. XXV, No 3. The story teaches that already in ancient times, just as in our days, the Vāṇiās allowed their daughters to learn to write, which accomplishment many Hindus still consider dangerous for female virtue.

communication from Dr. B. Liebich (p. 120 f.) has put me in possession of the proof that the Bengal schoolmasters until a very recent period used a set of twelve such tables, called *phalā* or in Sanskrit *phalaka,* which term the Chinese expressions *chang* and *fan* probably are intended to render.

Dr. Grierson's important researches at Mahābodhi Gayā, the results of which lately have been reprinted in the Proceedings of the Asiatic Society of Bengal, 1896, p. 52 ff., have made it necessary to rewrite the passage (p. 31 f.) on the remnants of the masons' alphabet, found there by Sir A. Cunningham, though the general conclusions to be drawn from them remain the same. A communication, kindly placed at my disposal by M. Sylvain Lévi, has furnished from Chinese sources a distinct tradition (p. 33), asserting that the signs for the liquid vowels really are later additions to the Brāhma alphabet, as the statement of the Jaina scriptures regarding the original number of its characters and the palaeographic evidence suggested. Mr. Rapson's discovery of syllables, both in Brāhmī and Kharoṣṭhī, on the Persian *sigloi* (pp. 51, 113) has further corroborated the conclusions regarding the early prevalence of both alphabets in Northwestern India and has raised a strong presumption that both alphabets were used in the same districts already in the fourth century B. C. during the Akhaemenian period. Finally, Mr. Takukusu's article on Pali Elements in Chinese has brought us the news that the tradition, asserting an early preservation of the Buddhist scriptures in MSS., is more ancient than the statement in the Life of Hiuen Tsiang could lead us to suppose, and nearly, if not quite as old as the contradictory statement of the Dīpavaṃsa and the Mahāvaṃsa (p. 91, note). And the most important discovery of a Kharoṣṭhī MS. at Khotan shows that during the Kuṣana period Buddhist MSS. did exist in Northern India and probably had been in use for some time (p. 122 f.).

While the new facts, contained in these recent contributions, have been duly utilised, it has not been possible to pay much attention to M. J. Halévy's two controversial papers in the Revue Sémitique of 1895, pp. 223 ff., 372 ff., beyond omitting in note 1 on p. 52 his derivation of the Brāhma numeral symbol for 8 (supposed to contain the first two letters of *aṣṭa*), from the Kharoṣṭhī *kha,* which, as he now tells us, is a misprint for *aś* (a non-existing and impossible ligature[1] originally invented by Dr. I. Taylor), and beyond adding a protest against the derivation of the circular cipher, which belongs not to the ancient Brāhma system of numeral symbols but to the later decimal notation, from the Kharoṣṭhī *da.*[2]

I regret that I have not been able to find in the two, somewhat excitedly written, articles any facts or suggestions, likely to benefit serious students of Indian antiquities. While repeating the ingenious, but extravagant, theories of the earlier paper, they teem in addition with statements which, though put forward with the author's characteristic apodictiveness and self-confidence, fill the Sanskritists rather with astonishment than with respectful admiration, and which fully justify their continued unwillingness to take his opinions on Indian matters into serious consideration. There is hardly a single subject of Indian research, on which they do not contain assertions, conflicting with perfectly well known and undisputed facts.

The quality of their scholarship and method is perhaps best illustrated by the results of the '*examen sérieux*' of the age of the Jātakas represented on the Stūpas of Sānchi and Bharahut,[3]

---

[1] The supposition that such a ligature is possible, betrays a want of acquaintance with the principles of Indian spelling. The Hindus divide *a-ṣṭa* (not *aṣ-ṭa*), *i-ṣṭa* (not *iṣ-ṭa*) *u-pta* (not *up-ta*) and so forth. Their ligatures represent elements of one and the same syllable, and hence they do not, and cannot, form ligatures like *aṣ* or *aś*, *iṣ*, *up* etc.

[2] It is a matter of course that M. Halévy sticks to the derivation of the Brāhma symbols for 4—9 from the Kharoṣṭhī initial letters of the Sanskrit numerals. The untoward fact that, except in the case of 5, either the supposed phonetical values or the forms of the signs do not agree with the requirements of the theory, is easily got over. The busy Gandharian inventors of the Brāhma symbols, we are told, had no time to look up Pāṇini, and so they put *cha* for *catuḥ* and so forth. Again if the contemporaneous forms of the symbols and the letters will not agree, those of different periods are chosen for comparison, and *e. g.* the Brāhma 6 of the 3rd cent. B. C. is declared to be a modification of the "cursive" Kharoṣṭhī *sa* of the 1st cent. B. C. The equally untoward fact that the Brāhma numeral signs include symbols for 20—100 and for 1000, which cannot be derived from Kharoṣṭhī letters, is carefully kept out of sight.

[3] Nouvelles Observations sur les Écritures Indiennes, p. 18f. (Revue Sém., p. 241 f.).

which, as it would lose in effect by curtailment, I translate in full:— "These monuments offer inscriptions in Aśoka characters; these insrs consequently cannot be earlier than B. C. 221, because otherwise the writing would run from the right to the left, as in the legend of the Eran coin. How far can the lower limit of their date go? Let us not put it too close to the relic caskets of Bhaṭṭiprolu, which are at least fifty years later, and which show already some altered forms, and let us put between the latter and the Stūpas an interval of twenty years. The inscriptions of Sanchi and Bharahut date therefore from about 191, *i. e*, one hundred and thirty four years later than the introduction of writing *(quaere, of the Brāhma letters?)* into India. It is in this interval that the composition *(sic)* must necessarily be placed, in the middle of the Greek epoch and in no way in the Persian period. Very luckily for us, the Katahaka-jataka *(sic)* mentions the writing-board, *phalaka*, and the texts of the Stūpas the canonical term *piṭaka* "a box for tablets of card-board or wood", in which the Jainas usually keep their MSS.,[1] with its derivative *peṭaki* "he who knows the Piṭaka or Piṭakas", where naturally not the box, but the tablets or leaves, contained in it, are meant. These are real revelations; for the terms *phalaka* and *piṭaka*, which have no etymology in Sanskrit,[2] are nothing but the Greek words πλαξ (-κός) and πιττάκιον;[3] the identity of sound corresponds to the identity of meaning. The Jatakas *(sic)* carry on their forehead

---

[1] "*Piṭaka* is only "a box" and corresponds to the modern *ḍābado* or card-board of wood *(sic)* in which the Jainas usually keep the MSS. of their parish libraries. (O. I. BA., p. 87.)"

[2] "The root *phal* 'to profit' gives birth to *phalaka* "profit, gain" and (metaphorically) "the catamenia", but does not explain the homophonous *phalaka* "board, *plaque* and tablet".

[3] "These two words have the identical meaning of "*plaque*" and "tablet". In Syriac פלקס is the same as לוחא (Duval, B. B., p. 1575) and פתקא (also very common in the Talmud) means "leaflet, leaf". Πιττάκιον is a popular word, which has come into literary use only rather late; but its antiquity is guaranteed by the proper name Πίτταχος *(sic)* borne by one of the Seven Sages of Greece, a contemporary of Solon. The word ἄσπρον "*un blanc*" presents an analogous case; though it has come late into literary use, one finds it once in an ancient decision of the Mišna (Ma'asêr šêni II אספרי כסף) and in the *Açpereno* of the Avesta."

the date of their birth, to wit, the century which follows the conquest of Alexander."

What occurs to a Sanskritist with regard to this remarkable statement of results, is as follows:—

(1) The assumption that all the Aśoka inscriptions date from B. C. 221, which is the basis of M. Halévy's contention that no inscription in Aśoka characters can be older than B. C. 221, and which is another version of his statement on p. 12, declaring the Aśoka edicts to have been incised about (*vers*) 221, is a sad blunder which a writer on Indian palaeography ought not to make. And it is the more unpardonable, as Professor Max Müller, whose Hibbert Lectures, translated by M. J. Darmesteter, M. Halévy quotes (p. 12, note 1) as his authority, explicitly gives B. C. 221 only as the date of the so-called three New Edicts of Sahasrām, Rūpnāth and Bairāt, following my calculations, and does not touch the question of the dates of the other numerous Aśoka inscriptions.

The dates of the incision of the following Aśoka inscriptions are clearly ascertainable and undisputed, (1) of the Barābar Hill Cave inscrs *A* and *B*, dated in Aśoka's 13th year, (2) of the Barābar H. C. inscr. *C*, dated in the 20th year, (3) of the Nigliva and Paḍeria pillar inscrs, dated in the 21st year, (4) of the first six so-called Pillar Edicts, dated in the 27th year, and (5) of the seventh edict on the Dehli-Sivalik pillar, dated in the 28th year. If Aśoka's coronation is fixed with Professor Max Müller in B. C. 259, these inscriptions range from B. C. 246—231; according to Professor Lassen's views they would fall each four years earlier, and according to Professor Kern, six years. As far as the evidence of the Aśoka edicts goes, the Sānchi and Bharahut inscriptions might, therefore, be placed at least a quarter of a century earlier than the 'examen sérieux' assumes.

(2) An undated fragment of an Aśoka edict, found on one of the broken gate-pillars of the Sānchi Stūpa, proves that the structure certainly existed before the end of that king's reign or, with Prof. Max Müller's initial date, before B. C. 222/21, and the presumption is that all the Sānchi inscriptions, showing Aśoka characters, were incised before that year. By the attempt to fix the erection of the Sānchi Stūpa between B. C.

221—191, M. Halévy collides with the clear epigraphic evidence, and commits a mistake which he might easily have avoided, if he had looked up the works on Sānchi. His attempt to drag down the age of the Bharahut Stūpa goes against the probability, as the inscriptions on the representations of the Jātakas show the same characters as the Aśoka edicts. All these representations thus give the reign of Aśoka as the *lower* limit for the *existence* of the Birth-stories. They teach nothing definite regarding the time of the composition of these fables, except in so far that they raise the presumption of their having been long current and generally known. For the archaeology of all nations proves that myths and scenes from religious legends are transferred to stone only when they have become thoroughly familiar to the people. Consequently, the assertion that the composition of the Jātakas must "necessarily" be placed between B. C. 221—191, is not warranted.

(3) M. Halévy's attempt to bring the Jātakas into the period after Alexander by deriving their term *phalaka* from the Greek πλὰξ and the word *piṭaka* (which itself does not occur "in the texts of the Stūpas") from πιττάκιον, only shows that his knowledge of Sanskrit is open to improvement and that he does not even take the trouble to consult the standard dictionaries. Both words are regular derivatives from Sanskrit roots. *Phalaka* "a board", comes from the very common verb *phal, (phalati)* "to split", mentioned in all Sanskrit dictionaries, and means etymologically "a piece (of wood) split off"; compare the Latin *scindula* from *scindo* and the Greek σχίδα, σχίδαξ, σχίζα from σχιδ (σχίζω). The etymology is duly given in the larger Petersburg Dictionary under *phalaka*. *Piṭaka* means primarily and usually "a basket" (used for any purpose, as for carrying earth, storing meat, measuring grain, etc.), more rarely "a box", as I have translated it, in which latter sense the cognate *peṭaka* is more common. Its employment to denote a receptacle for MSS., or the contents of such a receptacle, or a division of the sacred books, is mainly or entirely confined to Buddhistic literature. *Piṭaka* is derived from the Sanskrit root *piṭ* (*peṭati*) 'to heap up, to store', as the larger Petersburg Dictionary indicates under that verb, and it means etymologically "an implement for heaping up or storing (ob-

jects)". Whatever may be the truth about the age of the Jātakas, these two words are certainly useless for M. Halévy's purpose. The triumphant tone, with which he brings forward his supposed discoveries, and the display of misplaced learning in the notes, especially the appeal to king Pittakos' name in support of the antiquity of the ἰδιωτικώτερον term πιττάκιον, make the passage most amusing to every scholar, possessed of philological training.

To this specimen of M. Halévy's scholarship and method may be added another, found in his remarks on *Kebuka* (N. O. É. I, p. 56), where he lays down the law to a native Pali commentator. "*Kebuka*, he informs us, is the name of a place belonging to *Seruma*; the idea of the commentator that it is the name of a river has not the slightest foundation." And he then goes on to treat us to the ingenious conjecture that *Kebuka* is the Caucasus which, as he alleges, in Persian bears the name *Ḳabaḳ* or *Ḳabkh*, essentially corresponding to the Pali word. A Sanskritist who reads vs. 106 of the Jātaka, No. 327 (Fausböll, vol. III, p. 91):

Kathaṃ samuddaṃ patari kathaṃ patari Kebukam |
Kathaṃ satta samuddāni kathaṃ simbalim āruhi ‖

can only translate:—

"How didst thou cross the ocean, how didst thou cross *Kebuka*, how the seven oceans? How didst thou climb the cotton-tree?"

and recognises at once from the use of the verb *patari* "didst thou swim" or "cross in a boat", that *Kebuka* has something to do with water and can only denote a river, a lake, an ocean, or water in general. The Jātaka No. 539 fully confirms this inference, as it says explicitly, *kebukaṃ vuccati udakam*,[1] "*kebuka* means water".

If it were worth the while, the list of positive mistakes and more than hazardous speculations might be enlarged *ad infinitum* by examples from passages on Indian phonetics, epigraphy, antiquities, Dharma and so forth. Similar instances might also be adduced, where the papers show a weakness in

---

[1] Fausböll, The Jātakas, vol. VI, p. 42, l. 11; compare also vs. 133, p. 32, where *kebuka* is used to denote a tank.

other subjects, *e. g.* in Greek,[1] or collide with the statements of the Greek historians.[2] But what has been given, will be amply sufficient to convince even others than Sanskritists that a fuller discussion of their contents cannot serve any useful purpose.

Recent utterances of Professors O. Donner, Konow, Ludwig, Macdonell, Oldenberg, Windisch and others on writing in India and on the Indian alphabets make it apparent that the object, for which the Indian Studies No. III and its supplement were written, has been attained. Among the Sanskritists it is now more generally recognised that there are good reasons for believing that writing was practised in India long before Nearchus saw the Hindus write on cloth, prepared from their native cotton, and before another unnamed companion of Alexander, whose statements Q. Curtius has preserved, saw them use for the same purpose the tender inner bark of trees, *i. e.* the well known *bhūrja* from the Himālaya. Equally the conviction has become stronger that the Brāhmī is the most ancient Indian alphabet and that the development of the Kharoṣṭhī is one of the results of the Persian domination over Gandhāra and Sindh. The settlement of the general outlines of the enquiry, — to which belongs also the recognition of the fact that the Brāhmī is the alphabet of the Pandits and the Kharoṣṭhī a script of the clerks and men of business, similar in character to the simpler and defective Nāgarī, Lande, Ṭakkarī, Kāethī, Moḍī and Gujarātī which have been developed out of the more elaborate Brāhmī, some in later and some in earlier times, — is all that can be carried through for the present. The details of the derivation, which are particularly difficult in the case of the

[1] See e. g. N. O. É., Note 1 on p. 15, where we find the instructive sentence, "*D'ailleurs le nom* Ἰῶνες (sic), *et encore moins la forme non-contractée* Ἰαωνες (sic), *n'était plus usité au temps d'Alexandre comme désignation collective des Grecs* (sic)".

[2] See e. g. N. O. É. I, p. 60, where the establishment of an administration of the Macedonian type is asserted to have taken place about B. C. 330 in the countries west of India, though the Greeks give us the names of the Persians and other Orientals appointed by Alexander as his Satraps, who, as far as is known at present, were not forced to pass previously a Greek Civil Service examination.

Brāhmī with its forms, pointing partly to very archaic and partly to transitional North-Semitic characters, may at any moment require modifications on account of new epigraphic discoveries in India or in Western Asia. And important epigraphic discoveries will, no doubt, soon be made in India, since of late ancient sites have been identified, which were famous places of pilgrimage before the times of the Mauryas.

Table of Contents.

I.

Ever since Mr. J. Prinsep succeeded in deciphering the Edicts incised by order of the god-beloved king Piyadasi of Pāṭalīputra on the pillars and rocks of Eastern, Central and Western India, the attention of the European Orientalists has been directed to the question of the origin of their curious alphabet, which is the parent of all those now used from Cape Comorin to the Himalayas and of many others occurring beyond the confines of India proper. And, while there has been not much difference of opinion regarding the derivation of the second alphabet, in which Piyadasi's servants placarded their master's sermons in the Northwestern corner of his dominions, the views regarding the source of the more common characters have diverged very widely. There has been almost from the beginning a pretty general consensus that the alphabet of the Shābāzgarhī and Mansehra Edicts, called by the Europeans the Arian, Ariano-Pali, Bactro-Pali, Gandharian, Northwestern or Northern and by the Hindus *Kharoṣṭhī lipi*,[1] is, as the direction of its letters from the right to the left at once suggests, of Semitic origin, and that it has been derived from one of the later types of the Northeastern Semitic alphabet. But for the characters running from the left to the right, called by the Europeans Lāth, Southern, Indian Pali, Indian or Maurya and by the
[2] Hindus *Brāhmī lipi*, not less than five different derivations have been proposed, of which a detailed demonstration has been attempted. The number of general, more or less vague,

---

[1] Regarding the Hindu names of the two alphabets see below p. 23.

suggestions is even greater.[1] Leaving the latter aside, the five theories may be briefly stated as follows:—

(1) According to Sir A. Cunningham the Indian Pali or Brāhma alphabet, is an Indian invention and is based on a system of indigenous hieroglyphics;[2]

(2) According to Professor A. Weber it is derived directly from the oldest Phoenician alphabet;[3]

(3) According to Dr. Deecke it is descended from the Assyrian cuneiform characters through an ancient Southern Semitic alphabet, which was also the parent of the Himyaritic;[4]

(4) According to Dr. Isaac Taylor it comes from an alphabet of Southern Arabia, the parent of the Himyaritic;[5]

(5) According to M. J. Halévy it is of a composite character eight consonants having been taken directly from the Aramaic alphabet of the fourth century B. C., six consonants and two initial vowels as well as the medial vowels together with the Anusvāra from the Ariano-Pali or Kharoṣṭhī, and five from the Greek; and this hotch-potch is alleged to have been concocted about 325 B. C.[6]

It must, however, be noted that the first among these theories seems to have been almost given up by its chief advocate some time before his death. For in his last discussion of the Indian alphabet[7] Sir A. Cunningham says, "The origin of the Indian alphabet is still unsettled. According to Lassen, Dowson, Thomas and myself, its origin was indigenous, [3] that is, it was invented by the people of India. But continental scholars are generally in favour of its derivation from some unknown Western source", and in the sequel, after criticising the latest theory, which he takes to be that of Dr. Taylor, he adds,[8] "It seems not improbable that this old Indian

---

[1] See the exhaustive review of earlier opinions in Dr. R. N. Cust's Linguistic and Oriental Essays. Second series, pp. 27—52.

[2] Corpus Inscr. Indicarum, vol. I, p. 52 ff.

[3] Zeitschrift der Deutschen Morgenländischen Ges., Bd. X, 389 ff.; Indische Skizzen, p. 225—250.

[4] Zeitschrift der Deutschen Morg. Ges., Bd. XXXI, 598 ff.

[5] The Alphabet, vol. II, p. 314 ff.

[6] Journ. Asiatique, série VIII, tome VI (1885), p. 268 ff.

[7] Coins of Ancient India, p. 38 f.

[8] Op. cit., pag. 41. The italics are mine.

alphabet, when it was first framed *or adopted*, did not possess any cerebral letters." These utterances indicate that in 1891 Sir A. Cunningham himself no longer felt as certain of the soundness of his views as in 1876, when he wrote the introduction to the Corpus Inscriptionum Indicarum. As far as has become known, they have not gained of late any new adherents, and with the death of the illustrious archaeologist they have probably become entirely a matter of the past. Sir A. Cunningham himself has furnished a very strong argument in favour of the opposite theory by publishing, op. cit., Plate XI. 18, a coin from Eraṇ, which shows an inscription in Brāhma characters running from the right to the left. This is really the link, which was wanted in order to complete the chain of arguments, proving the Semitic origin of the Brāhma alphabet.

The remaining theories coincide in the main point that the ancient Indian characters are derived from a Semitic source, and Sir A. Cunningham is no doubt right, when he says that this is the prevailing belief among Sanskritists, not only however among those of the European continent, but pretty nearly all over the Western world. This belief is probably founded not so much on special studies in Indian palaeography, which, as well as epigraphy, are mostly neglected owing to the force of unfavourable circumstances, as on the general impression that certain Indian characters strongly resemble Semitic letters and on the conviction, supported in several cases by the clearest evidence, that the Indo-Aryan civilisation includes many and various elements, borrowed from Western nations, Semites, Persians and Greeks. But I doubt that even half a dozen Sanskritists could be found, who would care to make a definite choice between the rival theories, except in so far that they might be inclined to reject M. Halévy's ingenious, but untenable combinations, which rest on *a priori* improbable assumptions [4] and partly on errors regarding facts, and which in their final results, *e. g.* the conclusion that the Vedas were composed in the time of the Mauryas, disagree with all the lessons taught by Indo-Aryan research.[1]

[1] With respect to the statement, that M. Halévy's theory has not found much favour with Sanskritists, I would point to Professor A. Weber's remarks in his paper "Die Griechen in Indien", p. 17 (Sitz. Ber. der

My own attitude with respect to this problem has been for a long time exactly the same. During the last fifteen years, whilst I have devoted a portion of my time to early Indian epigraphy, it has been with me an open question whether the Brāhma characters came from western or from southern Asia. I have always believed in their Semitic origin. But I have vacillated more than once between their derivation from a pre-Himyaritic alphabet of Arabia and that from the ancient northern Semitic characters, which show almost identical forms in Palestine, Phoenicia, Cyprus and Assyria. And I have hesitated to take up the enquiry in real earnest, because it seemed to me that one preliminary condition to a new attempt on the problem was the preparation of perfectly trustworthy impressions and facsimiles of the oldest Indian inscriptions, and a second, the careful study of all these documents from a palaeographic and from a philological point of view. The first condition has now been fulfilled thanks to the unwearied labours of Messrs Burgess, Fleet, Führer, Hultzsch, Rice and Senart. Really good facsimiles of all the versions of the Edicts of Aśoka have been prepared and mostly published, as well as faithful reproductions of the closely allied, quite or nearly contemporaneous inscriptions in Daśaratha's caves, on the Bharhut or Bharaut and Sānchi Stūpas, on the Ghasundi slab, on the Sohgaurā Copper plate, in the Hathigumphā, Nānāghāt and Pabhosa caves. Moreover, the palaeographic store has been unexpectedly enriched by Mr. Rea's discoveries in the Bhaṭṭiprolu Stūpa, which have brought to light a new type of Brāhma characters, showing a certain independence, and, as it would seem to me on further consideration, at least some very archaic forms. The explanation of these [5] ancient documents, too, has so far advanced as is requisite for the palaeographic enquiry.

Under these circumstances I believe it possible to resume the discussion regarding the origin of the Brāhma alphabet with some hope of success, and I may state at once that the re-

---

Berliner Akademie, 1890, XXXVII), to Professor A. Ludwig's interesting paper on "Yavanānī", Sitz. Ber. der k. Böhm. Ges. der Wiss., 1893, No. IX, to Mr. S. Soerensen's Om Sanskrits Stilling i den almindelige Sprogudvikling i Indien, Copenhagen 1894, p. 288, note 1, and to Professor Kern's remarks in Dr. Cust's Essay's, p. 39.

sults, at which I have arrived in general confirm the views of Professor Weber, who has already given the correct identifications for the majority of the signs. In the case of most of the letters it is, of course, now possible to adduce forms which come closer to each other than those which his table contains. This is chiefly due to the numerous discoveries in Semitic epigraphy, which have been made during the last thirty nine years. Mesa's stone, the oldest Sinjirli inscription and the inscriptions on the Assyrian weights, which are datable more or less accurately, each furnish something valuable. And these discoveries make it also possible to adhere strictly to the general rule, to be observed in such inquiries, that only the signs of one period should be chosen for comparison.

Before I proceed to this comparison, it will be desirable to call attention to some passages in Indian literature, recently made accessible, and to some peculiarities in the oldest forms of the Brāhma alphabet, revealed by the new facsimiles and by a tabular arrangement of the signs, which I have lately undertaken for my „Grundriss der indischen Palaeographie".[1] Both the passages in the literary works and the characteristics of the oldest alphabet point to the conclusion that the Hindus extensively used the art of writing at least about three centuries before the time of Aśoka-Piyadasi.

II.

When thirty five years ago Professor Max Müller wrote his excursus on the Introduction of Writing in India,[2] the oldest Brahminical works which he could quote as witnesses for the use of letters were Pāṇini's Grammar, Manu's and Yājñavalkya's Institutes of the Sacred Law, the Mahābhārata and Kālidāsa's Dramas, and he had to declare that in the Vedas [6] and in the later literature of the Vedic schools no certain trace of the use of writing could he found, while they contained very strong evidence for the prevalence of oral teaching and for

---

[1] Grundriss der Indo-Arischen Philologie und Alterthumskunde, Bd. I, Heft 11, Strassburg i. E. 1896.

[2] History of Ancient Sanskrit Literature, p. 497 ff.

their having been preserved by a purely oral tradition. From the heterodox literature he was only able to adduce a passage of the Lalitavistara which describes the first visit of prince Siddhārtha, the future Buddha, to the writing school, and from non-Indian sources the seemingly conflicting utterances of Nearchos and of Megasthenes, one of the most careless reporters on Indian subjects. Professor Max Müller's final conclusion was, therefore, that the art of writing became known in India about 400 B. C. in the middle of his Sūtra-period and that, then and even later, it was not applied to literary purposes.

With the further exploration of Indian literature various additional pieces of evidence have come to light, which somewhat modify the above inferences and tend to show that writing was extensively used for the most various purposes at an earlier period. A closer scrutiny of the ancient Dharmasūtras has proved that there is at least one among them, the so-called Vāsiṣṭha Dharmaśāstra, which in general mentions written documents *(lekhya)* as a proof of ownership (XVI, 10) and enjoins in particular (XVI, 14—15) that in disputes about houses and fields the judicial decisions shall be given in accordance with the documents if the evidence of the neighbours disagrees, and that they shall be based on the statements of the old men and of the guilds, in case conflicting documents are produced.[1] Regarding the age of Vasiṣṭha's Institutes of the Sacred Law nothing definite is known. It is only possible to say that this work is a real Dharmasūtra, that it was originally composed for the use of the students of a northern school connected with the Ṛgveda and was considered to be of *general* authority before the eighth century of our era.[2] With respect to its relative position among the works on the sacred law, it is possible to assert that it is older than the famous Manusaṃhitā, where one of its rules is quoted and the name of its supposed author [7] is mentioned, while in its turn it quotes the ancient Dharmasūtra of the Mānavas, on which the homonymous metrical law-

---

[1] Sacred Books of the East, vol. XIV, p. XXVI and p. 80. The first-mentioned passage is a verse, quoted by the author either from the tradition of the learned or from an older work.

[2] Kumārila, Tantravārttika, p. 179, Benares edition.

book is founded.[1] It is also later than Gautama's Dharmasūtra and probably belongs to the period, when special law-schools had come into existence and taught the sacred and civil law in rivalry with the teachers of the Vedic schools. These circumstances make it difficult to deduce from its mention of written documents more than the obvious general conclusion that the art of writting was commonly used in daily life and its importance for legal purposes was recognised during the period, when new Vedic schools were still founded, and that it is erroneous to consider the admission of written documents as legal evidence to be a distinctive mark of the metrical manuals of the special law-schools. On general grounds it is probable that the composition of the Vāsiṣṭha Dharmaśāstra falls some centuries before the beginning of our era. To such a conclusion points *inter alia* the fact that it is older than our Manusaṃhitā. But for the present it would be hazardous to say anything more definite regarding its age.

More instructive are the numerous passages in the canonical works of the Southern Buddhists which testify to an extensive use of writing in very early times. All those sections of the Tripiṭaka, which contain descriptions of, or allusions to, the national life of ancient India, furnish some contribution to the subject. In the Jātakas, where, of course, most may be expected, most is also found. Private and official correspondence by means of letters is referred to again and again as something quite common. In the Kaṭāhaka Jātaka we are told how Kaṭāhaka, a slave of the Sheth, or great banker and merchant of Benares, by means of a forged letter passed himself off as the son of his master and obtained the daughter of the Sheth of another town:—

"He (Kaṭāhaka) who performed in the Sheth's house the work of a store-keeper thought, 'These people sha'nt make me always do the work of a store-keeper and treat me as a slave, striking, imprisoning and branding me, if they find fault with me. In a neighbouring kingdom there is a Sheth, a friend of [8] our Sheth. If I take to him a letter *(lekha)* written in our Sheth's name, and if I go to him and say that I am the Sheth's son, I

[1] Sacred Books of the East, vol. XXV, p. XXIX f.

may deceive him, obtain his daughter and live comfortably'. He himself took a leaf *(paṇṇa)*, wrote as follows, 'I have sent my son N. N. to thee; mutual connexion by marriage is suitable for us; give, therefore, thy daughter to this boy and let him live there; when I have time, I will also come', and he sealed the letter with the Sheth's seal. Then he took money for the journey, perfumes, clothes and so forth according to his pleasure, travelled to the neighbouring kingdom and stood before the Sheth there, respectfully saluting him. Then the Sheth asked him, 'Friend, whence hast thou come?' 'From Benares.' 'Whose son art thou?' 'The Benares Sheth's.' 'For what purpose hast thou come?' Thereupon Kaṭāhaka handed over the letter, saying, 'You will know it, when you have read this.' The Sheth read the letter, and exclaiming, 'Now I live indeed!', he gave him joyfully his daughter and established him there."[1]

Again the Mahāsutasoma Jātaka mentions a correspondence by means of letters *(paṇṇa)* between a teacher of Takkasilā and his former pupils,[2] and the Kāma Jātaka[3] narrates, how a prince, who had renounced the throne and lived in a village, was asked to write and actually wrote a letter *(paṇṇa)* to his brother, the reigning king, requesting a remission of the royal taxes for the people who had hospitably received him.[4]

An official letter is mentioned and its preparation is described in the Puṇṇanadī Jātaka,[5] which gives an account of the manner, in which the future Buddha was re-installed in his position as Purohita of the king of Benares, after having been banished in consequence of the intrigues of his enemies. "Afterwards the king remembered his *(the Bodhisattva's)* virtues, and reflected thus, 'It is not proper to send somebody in order to call my teacher; but I will compose a verse, write a [9] letter *(paṇṇa)*, order crow's flesh to be cooked, tie up the

---

[1] Fausböll, Jātakas, vol. I, p. 451, l. 22ff.

[2] Op. cit., vol. V, p. 458.

[3] Op. cit., vol. IV, p. 169.

[4] Compare also the Hārita Jātaka, No. 331, op. cit., vol. III, p. 498, l. 18, where the ministers send a *paṇṇa* to the king regarding Hārita's misconduct (reference kindly supplied by Prof. S. v. Oldenburg).

[5] Op. cit., vol. II, p. 173f.

letter *(paṇṇa)* and the flesh in white cloth, seal it with the royal seal *(rājamuddikā)* and send it to him. If he is clever, he will come after reading the letter and recognising the crow's flesh; if he is not clever, he wo'nt come'. He then wrote the verse, which begins with the words *puṇṇaṃ nadiṃ,* on a sheet." Of course the future Buddha was clever, and came back to Benares.

Further, some other passages mention official correspondence between kings. In the Cullakāliṅga Jātaka[1] we are told how powerful Kāliṅga, the king of Dantapura, eager for warfare, tried to pick a quarrel with the princes of India, whom he found disinclined to gratify his bellicose inclinations. In order to effect his purpose he sent his four beautiful daughters in a covered cart through the territories of his neighbours and ordered their guards to proclaim that any prince, who might take them into his harem, would have to fight their father. Assaka *(Aśmaka),* the king of Potali, dared to arrest their progress, and made all the four maidens his queens. Thereupon the Kāliṅga marched out with his army. But Nandisena, the minister of the Assaka king, the Jātaka continues, "hearing of his approach sent a royal decree *(sāsana)* to the following effect, 'Let him stop within the boundaries of his territory, let him not cross our frontier, *(else)* a fight will take place between the two kings'. When he *(the Kāliṅga)* had heard this letter read *(lekhaṃ sutvā),* he stopped within his own territory." Here the term *sāsana,* literally 'an order', is of considerable interest, as it is the representative of the Sanskrit *śāsana,* which occurs so frequently as the technical term for landgrants.[2]

Another case occurs in the Asadisa Jātaka,[3] according to which seven kings besieged the town of Benares and sent to Brahmadatta, its ruler, a letter *(paṇṇa),* asking him either to give up his kingdom or to fight. The future Buddha, who was then Prince Asadisa, king Brahmadatta's elder brother, came to the asistance of the latter. He cut *(achindi)* on an

---

[1] No. 301, op. cit., vol. III, p. 4 ff.

[2] Two other cases, in which letters, called *paṇṇa* and *sāsana,* are mentioned occur in No. 186, op. cit., vol. II, p. 104, l. l. 8 and 9, and No. 462, op. cit., vol. IV, p. 133, l. l. 4 and 9 (Oldenburg).

[3] No. 181, op. cit., vol. II, p. 89 ff.

arrow the following letters *(akkharāni)*: "I, Prince Asadisa, have come, and shall destroy with one arrow the lives of all [10] of you; let those fly who wish to live," and, being unrivalled in the archer's craft, he shot his arrow on the knob of the golden dinner-vessel of the besiegers. The latter, who where just sitting at dinner, read the letters and, of course, speedily raised the siege.

The Jātakas contain also a passage, mentioning the use of writing for legal purposes. In the Ruru Jātaka[1] a debtor invites his creditors to come with the bonds *(iṇapaṇṇāni)*, which he had given to them, to the banks of the Ganges in order to receive payment. The same Jātaka, (p. 257) mentions further the custom of inscribing particular important records or compositions on gold-plates. Khemā, the queen of Benares, had dreamt of a gold-coloured deer and had notified to her husband that she must die, if the deer was not found. The uxorious king composed this verse:—

"To whom shall I give a rich village and women decked with ornaments? Who will tell me of that deer, the best deer among deer?"

which he caused to be engraved on a gold-plate. The plate he made over to his prime minister and caused the inscription to be read to the townspeople.[2] While in this case the text engraved is a kind of proclamation, we learn from the Kaṇha Jātaka[3] that in rich families statements regarding the acquisition of property were preserved in this peculiar manner. The future Buddha, the story says, who had been born as the son af a Brahman possessing eighty millions, after the death of his parents "one day examined his treasury. Seated on a splendid couch, he caused a gold-plate to be brought and looked at the letters *(akkharāni)*, incised on it by his ancestors, which stated, 'So much wealth has been gained by such a one and so much by such another one'."

---

[1] No. 482, op. cit., vol. IV, p. 256.

[2] According to No. 159, op. cit., vol. II, p. 36, the king of Benares caused the information about a gold-coloured peacock to be engraved on a gold-plate, which one of his successors caused to be read out (Oldenburg).

[3] No. 440, op. cit., vol. IV, p. 7.

Three other cases, mentioned respectively in the Kurudhamma Jātaka,[1] the Tesakuna Jātaka and the Sambhava Jātaka are again different.[2] All three stories narrate, how particularly valued moral maxims were engraved on gold-plates apparently in order that they might [11] not be forgotten. In the first the inscription records at the king's command the Kurudhamma, the law of the Kurus, which is identical with the five great precepts, imposed by all Indian religions on laymen, 'Not to slay, not to steal, not to commit adultery, not to lie, not to drink intoxicating drinks.' According to the second story the future Buddha caused the *vinicchayadhamma* "the maxims concerning righteous judgment and the behaviour of kings", which he had preached, to be perpetuated in the same way.[3] In addition to these testimonies for the use of writing the Kaṭahaka Jātaka, already quoted, gives a hint regarding the existence of writing-schools and the manner in which writing was taught in ancient India. But, this had be better reserved for a fuller discussion of that subject.

Equally valuable are a number of passages of the Vinaya-piṭaka, which Professor Oldenberg's Index makes easily accessible. Writing *(lekhā)* and writers *(lekhaka)* are mentioned in the Bhikkhu Pācittiya II. 2 and in the Bhikhunī Pācittiya 49. 2. In the former passage writing is enumerated among "the excellent branches of learning, which are not blamed, nor despised, nor contemned, nor disregarded, *(but)* esteemed in the various countries." In the Pārājika section a curious practice is forbidden to the Buddhist monks, in which writing plays an important part. "*(If one)* cuts *(chindati)*, the text says, an inscription *(lekhaṃ)* to this effect, 'He who dies in this manner, will obtain wealth, or will obtain fame, or will go to heaven,' *(the cutter)* is guilty of a Dukkaṭa *(dushkṛta)* sin for each single letter *(akkharakkharāya)*. *(If anybody)* sees the inscrip-

---

[1] No. 276, op. cit., vol. II, pp. 371, 381.

[2] No. 522, op. cit., vol. V, p. 125, compare No. 515, op. cit., vol. V, p. 59 (Grierson).

[3] According to Jātaka No. 509, op. cit., vol. IV, p. 488 f., information about hidden treasure was written on gold-plates. The same story narrates that Viśvakarmā wrote with *jātihiṅgula* on the walls of the *paṇṇasālās* which he built by order of Indra (Oldenburg).

tion, and forms the painful resolution to die, *(the engraver will be guilty)* of a Thullaccaya *(sthūlātyaya)* sin; *(in case the reader actually)* dies, *(the engraver will be guilty)* of a Pārājika offence."[1]

The passage indicates that it was the practice of religious teachers to incite their lay-hearers by the promise of rewards in the next birth to commit suicide, and that they distributed tablets of wood or bamboo with inscriptions specifying the manner of the death and the rewards to be gained. The statement is perfectly credible, as religious suicide, or suicide with the hope of rewards in the next birth, was very common in ancient India and even occurred not rarely within [12] the last thirty or forty years.[2] The Dharmasūtras and the metrical Smṛtis mention the voluntary death by starvation or by other more violent means and even recommend it to the hermits and to the other ascetics,[3] and there are passages in the Mahābhārata, where ascetics, kings and others are recommended to put an end to their existence by starvation, jumping down from precipices, voluntary cremation and so forth. The Jainas were and are universally in favour of the 'death of the sages', though it has gone out of fashion in our days. And Hiwen Tsiang, Siyuki I, p. 232 (Beal) testifies to the prevalence of the belief that a jump from the Akṣaya Vaṭa, the sacred fig-tree at Allahabad, secured re-birth among the gods, as well as to the fact that it was acted on in the seventh century. Like the majority of the Brahminical teachers who, though giving the old rules, strongly disapprove of suicide, the Buddhists naturally opposed such practices. Their statement that written exhortations to suicide used to be given, furnishes another valuable piece of evidence for the very general use of writing in ancient India.

Finally there are still two remarkable passages in the Mahāvagga I, 43 and 49, which are also of considerable im-

---

[1] See also Prof. Oldenberg's remarks in Sacred Books of the East, vol. XIII, p. XXXII f.

[2] In January 1869 there was still a guard on the Girnār, in order to prevent pilgrims from jumping from the rock, called the *Bhairav jhāṁp* 'Bhairava's leap'.

[3] See Manu VI, 31 and the passages quoted in the Synopsis to my Translation, Sacred Books of the East, vol. XXV, pp. 204, 557.

portance for our question.[1] The first tells us that a *likhitako coro*, a thief whose name had been placarded or proclaimed in writing in the king's palace had been received into the order of the Buddhist monks. The people murmured against this and Buddha, of course, forbade for the future the admission of proclaimed thieves. The story confirms the hints, to be gathered from the Jātakas, regarding written royal proclamations. The second passage, which is literally reproduced in Bhikkhu Pācittiya 65. 1, and hence must be very ancient, describes in detail the deliberations of the parents of a boy of Rājagṛha, called Upāli, about their son's education. They agree that it would be beneficial for his future, if he learnt *lekhā* 'writing', *gaṇanā* 'arithmetic' and *rūpa*, literally 'forms'. But [13] they find that the first art might injure his hands, the second his chest and the third his eyes. Hence they finally resolve to permit him to enter the order of the Buddhist monks, who are of good moral conduct, dine well and sleep in well sheltered beds.

Even at first sight it seems probable that *rūpa, gaṇanā* and *lekhā* were the three "Rs", or subjects taught in the elementary schools of ancient India, when the Mahāvagga was composed. This conjecture is confirmed by a remark, which king Khāravela makes about his own education in the Hathigumphā inscription, dated in the year 165 of the Maurya era.[2] He says concerning himself:— पंदरवसानि सिरिकुमारसरीरवता कीडिता कुमारकीडिका [।] ततो लेखरूपगणनाववहारविधिविसारदेन सववजावदातेन नववसानि योवराजं पसासितं [॥]

"Endowed with the body of a glorious prince, he played during fifteen years children's games. Then, being expert in writing, *rūpa*, arithmetic and legal rules and excelling in all sciences, he ruled during nine years as Caesar."

Dr. Bhagvānlāl renders the untranslated word *rūpa* by "painting", while Professors Oldenberg and Rhys Davids, Sacred Books of the East, vol. XIII, p. 201, take it to mean in the Mahāvagga "money-changing", because Buddhaghoṣa says in the com-

---

[1] See also the remarks on these two stories by Prof. Oldenberg in Sacred Books of the East, vol. XIII, p. XXXIIf. and by D'Alwis, Introduction to Kachchhāyana's Grammar, pp. XXVII, CXVf., 73—101.

[2] Actes du VI. Congrès Int. Or. III, 2, p. 154.

mentary that "he who learns the *rūpa-sutta* must turn over and over many *kārṣāpaṇas* and look at them". The rendering "money-changing", though not far from the truth, is a little too specific. For it is not probable that a royal prince would qualify himself to become a banker. But, the curriculum of the so-called indigenous schools of the present day includes a branch of elementary learning, which may be called *rūpa* "forms" and to which Buddhaghoṣa's explanation may also refer.[1] After the children have mastered the art of writing and the most elementary arithmetical operations, addition, subtraction and particularly the *āṃk* or complicated multiplication tables, they are instructed in the practical application of arithmetic [14] to simple commercial and agricultural affairs. They learn, how many Ḍāms, Korīs, Pāisās, Pāulās and so forth go to the Rupee, the rules for calculating interest and wages as well as the simplest rules of mensuration.[2] This commercial and agricultural arithmetic is no doubt what is meant by *rūpa* and it may be that in ancient times, when coins were rare, specimens were placed before the pupils, which they had to handle and look at, in order to learn their form, weight and marks. As far as I am aware, this is not done in our days.[3]

With respect to the instruction in writing, there is, as stated above, something more in the beginning of the Kaṭāhaka Jātaka. "When the son of the Sheth, the story says, learnt writing, the slave (Kaṭāhaka) too went with him carrying his

---

[1] My statements regarding the indigenous schools are based on what I have seen in Western, Northern and Central India. The Rev. J. Long's edition of Adam's Reports on Vernacular Education, pp. 19ff. and 98ff. furnishes confirmatory statements. See also Captain Harkness' article on the schools in Southern India, Jour. Roy. As. Soc., vol. I, p. 15f., Mr. Gover's on the Dyal schools of Madras, Indian Antiquary, vol. II, p. 52ff., and Mr. Raghunāthjī's on the Marāṭhī schools, Indian Antiquary, vol. VIII, p. 246ff.

[2] What is taught in this way in the indigenous schools of Gujarāt has been collected by Rao Saheb Bhogilāl Prāṇvallabh and published by the Bombay Educational Department under the title *Desī Hisāb*, "Native Arithmetic", Pts. I and II.

[3] According to Major Temple the Burmese market-girls were actually taught in this way within the last thirty years, Indian Antiquary, vol. XXIV, p. 247, Notes.

board and *(thus)* learnt writing." The sentence indicates, that the Sheth's son did not receive instruction at home, but went to a master, who presumably kept a school. The mention of the "board" *(phalaka)* is very interesting. It agrees with the narrative of the Northern Buddhist Lalitavistara, according to which young Siddhārtha, the future Buddha, on going to the school of the Brahman Viśvāmitra, brought with him "a golden pencil and a tablet of red sandal wood".[1] And the actualities in the indigenous schools of Western, Northern, Central and Eastern India[2] furnish the necessary commentary on the two passages. Nearly everywhere the board or wooden tablet is still in use for the first instruction in writing, and it is either covered with sand in which the letters are drawn with a small stick, or it is varnished and the letters are drawn with a stick, smeared with a solution of white chalk instead of ink.[3] It is [15] evident that the Lalitavistara and the Jātaka refer to the method of instruction, which is still followed, and the information, conveyed by the latter and Mahāvagga I. 49, makes it probable that elementary schools existed at the period, when the Buddhist canon was composed, and that their curriculum was about the same as that of the indigenous Pāṭhśālās, Lehsaḍs, Nīśāḷs (*i. e.* *Lihśālās) and Tolls of modern India.

In the portions of the Nikāyas, which I have read, I have met with fewer references to writing. But they are not entirely

---

1 Professor Terrien de la Couperie, Babylonian and Or. Record, vol. I, p. 59, states that these words are found in the older Chinese translation, Pu yao king, dated 308 A. D. The legend possibly goes back to the beginning of our era.

2 Regarding Bengal and Behar, see the passages from Adam's Report quoted above.

3 In Gujarāt the latter method is the more common one, and a vessel, filled with a solution of chalk usually belongs to the paraphernalia of the schoolboys. But I have likewise seen the sanded board, on which the grains are made to adhere slightly by gum arabic. Very poor boys simply scattered dust on their boards and wrote in that, or if they had no boards, they brought brass kettles or pans and wrote on these with chalk. This happened even in the Government schools, where more usually slates and chalk-solution were used by the beginners or Āṃkvālās, as the school-phrase is. Bērūnī, India, vol. I, p. 182 (Sachau), writing in A. D. 1030, mentions the use of black tablets in the schools, on which the children wrote with a white material.

wanting. Thus the Brahmajāla Sutta 14 and the Sāmaññaphala 49, mention a game, called *akkharikā*,[1] which according to Buddhaghoṣa means "reading letters in the air or in the vault of the sky", see also Childers, Pali Dict. s. v. *piṭṭhī*.

As regards the question to which exact period the testimony of the Pali Canon may refer, the answer, I think, must be, "to the fifth and possibly to the sixth century B. C." In the introduction to the Vinayapiṭaka Professor Oldenberg has shown that there are good reasons for assuming the composition of the Mahāvagga, Pācittiya and Pārājika sections to precede the Council of Vesālī (ca. 380 B. C.) and to fall even somewhat earlier than the year 400 B. C.[2] While it will be sufficient to refer to his discussion on the Vinaya and to Professor M. Müller's review of the question in the introduction to the Dhammapada, Sacred Books of the East, vol. X, p. XXIX ff., the case of the Jātakas requires a fuller consideration.

It is a well known fact that the sculptures on the Sānchi and Bharahut or Bharaut Stūpas contain representations of various Jātakas. On the Sānchi Stūpa the Sāma Jātaka has been identified[3] and others, like the Mahākapi Jātaka, may be recognised even on the Plates in Dr. Fergusson's Tree and Serpent [16] Worship. On the Bharahut Stūpa twenty-one sculptured scenes, to which the titles are mostly added, have been found to correspond with Birth Stories in Professor Fausböll's printed edition, and Dr. E. Hultzsch has shown that even a Pāda of a verse, used as a title, agrees with the printed text.[4] Among

---

[1] Mentioned also in the Cullavagga I, 13. 2 and elsewhere.

[2] Vinayapiṭaka, vol. I, p. XXXIV—XXXVIII.

[3] Jour. Roy. As. Soc. 1894, p. 211 ff.

[4] Indian Antiquary, vol. XXI, p. 225 f., where Dr. Hultzsch has reprinted his excellent edition of the inscriptions together with a synopsis of the stories hitherto identified and other very valuable remarks. The fact that the titles of the stories frequently differ, the Pali text naming the story after one chief actor or incident and the inscription after another, has been discussed by Professor Rhys Davids in the Introduction to his Buddhist Birthstories p. LX ff. And he has shown that it in no way goes against the assumption that the canonical collection existed at the time when the sculptures were made, because vacillations with respect to the titles occur likewise in the Pāli collection. I would add that variations in titles are also found in Brahminical literature. Thus Bāṇa

them there are also two, the Rurumiga and the Asadisa, which have been quoted above as witnesses for the use of writing. Both the Stūpas date from the third century B. C., some additions only belonging to the second century. The age of the Sānchi Stūpa is proved by a fragment of an Aśoka Edict, which agrees in part with the so-called Kosambī Edict on the Allahabad Pillar, and by the fact that the characters of more than nine tenth of its nearly four hundred inscriptions fully agree with those of the Aśoka Edicts, while about two score show slightly more advanced forms.[1] Similarly, nearly all the hundred and fifty three published inscriptions of the Bharahut Stūpa are written in the alphabet of the Edicts, and it is chiefly Dhanabhūti's inscription on the gateway-pillar dated "in the reign of the Śuṅgas", which is incised in more modern letters. The pieces with the later characters are, of course, additions or repairs, made [17] after the completion of the original structure.[2] Under these circumstances it is very probable that in the third century B. C. our collection of the Jātakas formed part of the Buddhist Canon, which, as the Bairat Edict, addressed to the Māgadha Saṅgha, and various inscriptions on the Stūpas indicate, was then fully settled. Both on the Sānchi and Bharahut Stūpas we read of monks who had the title *pacanekāyika (pāñcanai-*

---

calls the Bhagavadgītā, Anantagītā. Kumārila uses the title Āścarya Parvan for the Putradarśana Parvan of the MSS. of the Mahābhārata, and there are Vedic hymns with two or three names. Such a vacillation comes quite natural to a Hindu, who is accustomed to substitute endless synonyms for technical terms and names of plants animals etc., and even changes portions of personal names, saying Vikramāditya, Vikramārka or Vikramāṅka, though he means the same individual. The discrepancies between the Pali stories and the representations in Bharahut, which Prof. Minayeff believed to have discovered (Recherches I, 140ff.), are, I think, merely such as may be expected to be found between all narratives and their illustrations by sculptures.

[1] See my articles on the Sānchi Stūpa inscriptions in the Epigraphia Indica, vol. II, p. 87ff. and p. 366ff., which latter is accompanied by two plates, giving specimens of inscriptions in the old and the more advanced characters.

[2] See the Plate in vol. XL of the Zeitschrift der Deutschen Morgenländischen Gesellschaft, and Indian Antiquary, vol. XIV, p. 139. The inscription of Dhanabhūti on the gateway-pillar belongs in my opinion to the middle of the second century B. C.

kāyika)[1] *i. e.* 'teacher of the five Nikāyas', and in Bharahut appears also a *peṭaki i. e.* 'a person who knew or taught the Piṭaka or Piṭakas', about whose designation more will be said below.

The evidence of the relievos on the Stūpas furnishes a lower date for the Jātakas, later than which their use for the edification of the Buddhist laymen cannot be put. But there are other circumstances connected with them, which make it very probable, that the picture of the national life of [18] India, furnished by them, refers to a much earlier period than the third century B. C. Though, as Professor Rhys Davids has shown op. cit., p. LV. ff., nothing definite is known regarding the date when the present collection was formed and incorporated in the Buddhist canon, it is already now evident that the stories which they contain are not, as was believed formerly, inventions of the Buddhist monks, but almost throughout loans from the ancient Brahminical literature or the old pre-Buddhistic national tradition of India. A very good statement of this view by Dr. S. von Oldenburg has been translated in

---

[1] By an oversight I have given in the Epigraphia Indica, vol. II, p. 93, *pañcanaikāyika* as the Sanskrit equivalent of *pacanekāyika*. Though such a form might be defended by analogous compounds like *tridrauṇika,* it is equally possible and no doubt better to assume that the prototype of the Prakrit word was formed in accordance with the rule, exemplified by *cāturvaidyaka* 'one who knows or teaches the four Vedas'. For, in the ancient epigraphic Prakrits *pañca* and *pāñca* would both be represented by *paṃca* or *paca* i. e. *pacca.* These remarks may possibly meet the doubts, which M. A. Barth has expressed regarding the word in the Bulletin des Religions de l'Inde, 1894, Bouddhisme, p. 1, note 1. M. A. Barth's further doubts, whether the five Nikāyas, known in the third century B. C., may be identified with those of the Pali Canon, do not appear justified to me. Assuming the correctness of his statement that the 'five Nikāyas' are unknown to the Northern Buddhists, this fact would, in my opinion, not prove anything *against* the antiquity of these collections, because the Northern Buddhists have preserved only the *disjecta membra* of an old tradition. No doubt, when the Northerners and the Southerners agree with respect to a particular text or collection, its great age is clearly established. But it seems to me dangerous to invert the proposition and to allege that books or collections of the Southern Canon, not known to the Northerners, must be considered later additions for this reason alone.

the Jour. Roy. As. Soc. of 1893, p. 301 ff., and I can only say that a closer study of the Jātakas had led me to the same conclusion before the publication of Dr. von Oldenburg's paper. Moreover, the detailed researches of Professor Leumann and of Dr. R. G. Bhāṇḍārkar have yielded exactly the same results, see the Wiener Zeitschrift für d. Kunde d. Morg. Vol. V, p. 111 ff., the Zeitschrift der Deutschen Morg. Gesellschaft Vol. XLVIII, p. 65 ff. and the Transactions of the IXth Int. Or. Congress, 1892, Vol. I, p. 422 ff.

This discovery makes the question regarding the exact date, at which the loan may have been effected, a matter of minor importance. The chief point for consideration is, if in effecting the loan the Buddhist monks altered much and especially, if the description of Indian life which the Jātakas contain, has been made to agree with that of the times when Buddhism had become a power in India. The answer can only be, that there are remarkably few traces of Buddhism in these stories and that they do not describe the condition of India in the third or fourth century B. C., but an older one. Peculiarly Buddhistic are only the introduction of the future Buddha into most tales, who invariably is identified with the wisest and best of the actors, occasional spiteful remarks against the Vedic animal sacrifices and against the deified national heroes, whom the orthodox sects worshipped, and intentional perversions of the legends told of them. The doctrine of the power of the Karman, the moral maxims and the few religious observances such as the sanctification of the Uposatha or Parvan days, which the stories inculcate, are common to the Buddhists and to all other Indian religions, whether orthodox or heterodox. [19] With respect to these there was not much to change, except perhaps some of the technical expressions.

On the other hand the descriptions of the political, religious and social condition of the people clearly refer to the ancient time before the rise of the great Eastern dynasties of the Nandas and the Mauryas, when Pāṭaliputra had become the capital of India. The Jātakas mention neither the one nor the other, and they know nothing of great empires which comprised the whole or large parts of India. The number of the kingdoms, whose rulers play a part in the stories, is very considerable. The majority of the names, such as Madra, the two Pañcālas, Kosala, Videha, Kāśi, and Vidarbha agrees with those mentioned in the Vedic literature, while a few others, like Kaliṅga and Assaka *i. e.* Aśmaka or Aśvaka, occur in Brahminical literature first in the Epics and in Pāṇini's Sūtras. The characteristic names of the Andhras, the Pāṇḍyas and Keralas are not mentioned.

Though a political centre was wanting, frequent statements regarding the instruction of the young Brahmans and nobles show that there was an intellectual centre and that it lay in Takkasilā, the capital of distant Gandhāra. Takkasilā is according to the Jātakas the town, where the youth of the two highest classes received instruction in the three Vedas and the twelve or eighteen branches of learning *(sippa* or *vijjāṭhāna)*. This agrees with some statements in other parts of the Canon, where, as in the Vinayapiṭaka, the famous physician Jīvaka Komārabhacca is represented as having studied medicine in Takkasilā. And it is very credible that Gandhāra, the native country of Pāṇini, was a stronghold of Brahminical learning certainly in the fourth and fifth centuries B. C., and perhaps even earlier.

The statements regarding the religious condition of India point to an equally early period. Just as the three Vedas are the basis of the higher instruction, so the prevalent religion is that of the Path of Works with its ceremonies and sacrifices, among which several like the Vācapeyya *(vājapeya)* and the Rājasūya are specially and repeatedly mentioned. Side by side with these appear popular festivals, celebrated, when the Nakṣatra had been proclaimed, with general merry-makings and copious libations of Surā, as well as the worship of demons and trees, [20] all of which go back to the earliest times. Nor are the hermits in the woods and the wandering ascetics unknown. Most of the heroes take the *isipabbajjā, i. e.,* renounce the world according to the rule of the Ṛṣis, and live with their sacred fires in the hill-forests, whence they descend occasionally in order to procure salt and pungent condiments *(loṇambilasevanattha)*. The wandering ascetics *(tāpasa)* appear to belong to different orders, as various distinctive marks are mentioned. But only those of one division, the Ājīvikas, are actually named, among whom the future Buddha himself was once born in a former Kalpa. These are, as Professor Kern has first pointed out, the ancient Vaiṣṇava devotees of Nārāyaṇa and particularly the Paramahaṃsas, who according to the lately recovered Vaikhānasa Dharmasūtra actually went naked and swallowed cowdung, as the Buddhists allege of these dangerous rivals.

The state of civilisation, described in the Jātakas, is in various respects primitive, and particularly noteworthy is the prevalence of wood architecture, which on the evidence of the oldest sculptures had almost disappeared in the third century B. C. The Jātakas even describe the palaces of kings as usually constructed of wood. Many other details might be added. But the facts given are sufficient for our purpose. They make it at least probable that the mention of writing as common in daily life is not an addition, made by the Buddhists in later times, but occurred in the old stories which they appropriated. And it ought to be remembered, that in the Puṇṇanadī and Asadisa Jātakas writing is not merely an ornamental accessory, but a most essential point, without which the stories would have no meaning, and that the Asadisa Jātaka is found on the Stūpa of Bharahut.

An additional argument for the antiquity of the writing, mentioned in the books of the Pali Canon, is furnished by the technical terms which they employ. They exclusively use for writing, writers and letters words which mean "to cut", *chind,* "to scratch" *likh,* "the scratcher" *lekhaka,* "scratching" or "scratches", *lekha,* and "the indelible" *akkhara.* On the other hand the word *lipi,* which Pāṇini, circiter 350 B. C.,[1] has in the compounds [21] *lipikara* and *libikara,* "writer", is not found in the Buddhist canonical works known to me, nor is there in Childers' Dictionary any quotation for it from the Canon. For *lipi* two explanations have been proposed. According to the older opinion it is de-

[1] I can only adhere to the traditional date of the great grammarian, which, as we know now, was contained in the ancient Bṛhatkathā, since both Kṣemendra's and Somadeva's Sanskrit translations contain the story of Pāṇini, the pupil of Upavarṣa, who flourished during the reign of Yogananda, the predecessor of Candragupta, Indian Antiquary, vol. I, p. 305. — Pāṇini's Dhātupāṭha gives for the verb *likh* the meaning *akṣaravinyāsa* 'arranging letters' or 'syllables' and thus furnishes, as Geheimrath von Böhtlingk points out to me, another proof for the prevalence of writing in the fourth cent. B. C.

rived from *lip* 'to smear', like *kṛṣi* 'agriculture' from *kṛṣ* 'to plough', and like a number of other substantives formed by the feminine affix *i*. According to others,[1] it is a corruption of the Old Persian *dipi* 'writing', which corruption was favoured by a fancied connexion with the verb *lip*. Though *lipi* might be a perfectly regular derivative from *lip*, and might appropriately have been used to denote 'letters' and 'the alphabet' on the introduction of writing with ink, the derivation becomes doubtful through the fact that the verb *limpati* is not used in the sense of 'he writes'. And the impressions of the Shāhbāzgarhī version of Aśoka's Edicts have furnished a strong argument for the adherents of the second view. For they show that in the Gandhāra dialect *lipi* is represented by *dipi* and that the verbs *dipati* 'he writes' and *dipapati* 'he causes to write' did also exist.[2] On linguistic grounds it is not probable that *lipi* and *limpati* should have been turned into *dipi* and *dipati*, the latter also changing its meaning. On the other hand, *dipi* corresponds exactly with the Persian word, and its introduction into India is easily explained by the Persian occupation of Northwestern India during the Akhaemenian period from about 500 B. C. probably until the fall of the Persian empire.[3] These points appear to me so strong that I too must declare myself in favour of the loan theory, and assume that in Sanskrit *lipi* was substituted for *dipi* at a period, when writing with ink had come into use, in order to connect the term with the [22] root *lip*. The statement of Nearchos, according to which the Hindus wrote letters ἐν σινδόσι λίαν κεκροτημέναις, as well as that of Q. Curtius VIII, 9, according to which they used *libri arborum teneri* i. e. birch-bark, for the same purpose, makes the use of ink certain for the latter half of the fourth century.[4]

---

[1] See, Burnell, Elements of South Ind. Palaeography, p. 5f., Note 2.

[2] The aorist *dipista* is found in Shāhbāzgarhi Ed. IV, l. 10; VI, l. 16 and the participle *dipapita ibidem*, Ed. XIV, l. 13.

[3] See also App. I, p. 95. It may be noted, that even in later times the Hindus have borrowed a Persian word, connected with writing. This is the term *divīra* — *divira*, "a writer, clerk", found in the Valabhī land grants of the seventh century A. D. and in later Kaśmīrian works. It represents the Persian *debīr*, see the smaller Petersburg Dictionary sub voce *divira*.

[4] The oldest preserved specimen of writing in ink occurs on the relic vase from Andher, Cunningham, Bhilsa Topes, Pl. 30, No. 6.

The loan theory agrees also well with the occurrence of the word in the Sūtras of Pāṇini, who was a native of Sālāturā, the modern village of Lahul, close to Ohind and west of the Indus, and with its absence from the ancient Buddhist canonical works, which were composed in Eastern India and before 400 B. C.

Some further valuable information regarding writing and especially regarding the ancient alphabets, is furnished by the works of the Northern Buddhists, by the Jaina scriptures and by some metrical Smṛtis. In the account of prince Siddhārtha's first visit to the writing-school, extracted by Professor Terrien de la Couperie from the Chinese translation of the Lalitavistara of 308 A. D. (see above p. 15, note 2), there occurs besides the mention of the sixty four alphabets, known also from the printed Sanskrit text, the utterance of the master Viśvāmitra, "that there are two kinds of writing, that of Fan or Brahman and that of Kuliu, both equally good and not differing". With the help of a Chinese Buddhist Encyclopedia, dated 668 A. D., Professor Terrien de la Couperie has shown that the alphabet of Brahman was written from the left to the right and that, invented by Kuliu, Kiülü, Kialu or Kialusheta (all of which names are explained by "ass' lips", in Sanskrit *kharoṣṭha*) from the right to the left. He thereby has rendered us the great service of showing what the terms Brāhmī and Kharoṣṭhī really mean. The former is evidently the alphabet, which used to be called Pali, Lāth, Southern Indian, Aśoka or Maurya, and the latter the so-called Northwestern, Ariano-Pali, Bactro Pali, or Gandhārian. With this explanation, the remark of the future Buddha's writing-master indicates, that at the time, when the Lalitavistara, translated into Chinese in 308 A. D., was composed, *i. e.*, at the latest in the third century A. D., both the ordinary Indian and the Gandhāra alphabets were equally common in the author's native country. If, as is not improbable on account of the position of the Lalitavistara in the Canon of the Northern Buddhists, this was the Panjab or one of the adjoining districts of Northwestern India, the statement agrees with the facts known through the inscriptions and coins, which [23] from the earliest times of the historical period of India until the end of the second century A. D., show both the Brāhma and Kharoṣṭhī characters.

The enumeration of the sixty-four alphabets[1] has gained a greater interest by the discovery of a similar, apparently independent list in the Jaina Āgamas. Professor Weber's analysis of the latter shows,[2] that they too allege the early existence of a larger number of scripts and that some of the names agree literally, or at least in meaning, with those given by the Buddhists. Both the Jainas and the Buddhists agree in allotting the first place, to "Brahman's writing", the *Brāhmī lipi* or *Bambhī livī*, indicating thereby the pre-eminence of the characters, running from the left to the right, which are used in the majority of Aśoka's Edicts. Both name also the alphabet written from the right to the left, which in the Jaina Prakrit is called *Kharoṭṭhī* instead of *Kharoṣṭhī*. Its position in the two lists somewhat differs, as the Buddhists give it the second place and the Jainas only the fourth. Further, both lists include the *Puṣkarasārī* (No. 3) or *Pukkharasāriya* (No. 5) and the *Drāviḍa* (No. 12) or *Ḍāmila* (No. 17) characters. The mention of the last alphabet has become important since the discovery of an ancient partly independent variant of the Brāhmī lipi at Bhaṭṭiprolu in the Kistna districts of the Madras Presidency. And it is not improbable that this alphabet is meant by "the writing of the Dravidian country[3]". The mention of the *Puṣkarasārī* or *Pukkharasāriyā lipi,* too, possesses some interest, as its name is evidently derived from the patronymic *Pauṣkarasādi* or *Puṣkarasādi,* which appears in Brahminical works on grammar and law as the designation of one, or perhaps of several famous teachers. It is certainly a Brahminical name and indicates that a scion of the race of *Puṣkarasad* invented some particular alphabet or introduced modifications [24] in an existing one. The name, therefore, furnishes the

---

[1] See Lalitavistara, p. 143 f. Calc. ed.

[2] Indische Studien, vol. XVI, pp. 280, 399 ff. The list occurs twice, in the Samavāyāṅga and the Paṇṇāvanā Sūtras. There is a third list of alphabets with about 30 mostly very corrupt names in the Mahâvastu, I, p. 135 (Senart), which has been omitted intentionally, as its exact contents cannot be made out with certainty.

[3] I may state here that in my opinion Dr. Burnell's contention for the antiquity of the Vaṭṭeḷuttu or Pāṇḍya-Cera alphabet is erroneous; see the Grundriss der Indo-Ar. Phil. und Alt., I, 11, § 32.

proof that in early times Brahmans directed their attention to the art of writing, for which view other arguments will be adduced further on. The other names, which like the *Gandharva* or *Gandhavva* agree fully, or like the *nāgalipi* "the writing of the snake-deities" and the *Bhogāvaiyā*, "the writing of Bhogāvatī, the residence of the Nāgas", in their general meaning, are perhaps in part fanciful and, at least for the present, not particularly instructive.

The independence of the Jaina list from that of the Lalitavistara is proved by various discrepancies. First, it is much shorter and includes only eighteen varieties, and among them occurs the *Javaṇāliyā* or according to the printed edition of the Paṇṇāvanā Sūtra, the *Javaṇāniyā*, which corresponds to Pāṇini's term *Yavanānī*,[1] or, as Kātyāyana's Vārttika states, "the writing of the Yavanas". Secondly, the Jainas use the term Bambhī livī in a double sense, not only for a particular variety of writing, but also for every kind of writing. The texts are explicit on this point and say,[2] *Baṃbhīe naṃ livīe aṭṭhārasavihalikkhavihāṇe paṇṇatte* | *taṃ baṃbhī* etc. "An eighteenfold order of scripts is taught for the Brāhma writing, viz. the Brāhma" etc. This apparently senseless assertion finds its explanation through passages of the metrical Smṛtis of Nārada and Bṛhaspati, as well as through Brahminical sculptures and pictures of Brahman. The two lawbooks state that "the Creator (Brahman) created writing in order to keep the affairs of the world in their proper course" or "in order to remove doubts regarding legal transactions".[3] On the sculptures in the Bā-

[1] The identification, which is given by Malayagiri, is unobjectionable, even if *Javaṇāliyā* is the correct form. For instances of the substitution of *la* for Sanskrit *na* occur *e. g.* in Pali *anela* for *anenas*, *muḷāla* for *mṛṇāla*, *veḷu* for *veṇu* and in Mahārāṣṭrī *velu* for *veṇu* and *limba* for *nimba*. It may be noted that the later Tibetan version of the Lalitavistara includes the *Yavanānī* in its list of seventy alphabets, see Foucaux, Rgya Cher Rol Pa, p. 112 f., and that the *Yonāri* of the Mahâvastu, loc. cit., is probably a representative of *Yavanānī* or *Yavanāli*.

[2] See A. Weber, op. cit., p. 399.

[3] Sacred Books of the East, vol. XXXIII, pp. 58 f., p. 304. Nārada's lawbook is later than the Manusaṁhitā and older than Bāṇa (circiter 620 A. D.), who alludes to it in the Kādambarī, p. 91 (Peterson). The Bṛhaspati Smṛti is again later than Nārada's.

[25] dāmī caves,[1] which date from the end of the sixth century A. D., the same idea is expressed by representing Brahman with strips of palmleaves in his right hand, for which modern pictures of the deity substitute an inscribed piece of paper.[2] It thus appears that there were two legends which the Jainas have combined, one which ascribed to Brahman the invention of all writing and another which restricted his activity to one particular alphabet, that which was the commonest and most generally used. Both myths no doubt were current side by side, and express with a slight variation the belief that writing is a national Indian invention.

These points, to which the differences in half a dozen names of alphabets must be added, show very clearly that the Jaina list has not been copied from that of the Buddhists, but gives expression to an independent tradition, which in all probability is considerably older than that of the Buddhists. The greater antiquity of the Jaina list is apparent from its more reasonable number of alphabets, which, however, is also a purely conventional one[3] and need not be taken to mean more than "a large number". It is also probable, because the Aṅga and the Upāṅga, in which it occurs, certainly are much older than the third century A. D., the time for which the existence of the Buddhist list is absolutely certain. In my opinion we have, since the discoveries in the Kankālī Tīla at Mathurā, very good reasons for believing the Śvetāmbara tradition which places the first collection of the Aṅgas in the reign of the Maurya Candragupta or about 300 B. C.[4] And, though the Aṅgas evidently have undergone changes between that time and their final redaction by Devarddhi in the fifth century A. D., it seems to me probable that the list of the alphabets belongs to the original contents of the Samavāyāṅga, because it has been embodied also in the Paṇṇāvaṇā Sūtra, the traditional date of which is 358 after Vīra or 168 B. C. Nor is the existence of such

---

[1] Indian Antiquary, vol. VI, plate facing p. 361.

[2] Moore, Hindu Pantheon, plate I, and the representation of Brahman in Sir W. Jones' article, Asiatic Researches, I, p. 222 ff.

[3] Compare the eighteen Purāṇas, and Upapurāṇas, the eighteen Smṛtis and Upasmṛtis.

[4] See Sacred Books of the East, vol. XXII, p. XL ff.

[26] a traditional list at the beginning of the Maurya period *a priori* incredible. Pāṇini's rule regarding the formation of *Yavanānī* "the writing of the Yavanas" very probably indicates, as has already been remarked by others, that in his time, *i. e.*, about 350 B. C., more alphabets than one were known,[1] and for the third century B. C. the contemporaneous use of three alphabets, the ordinary Brāhmī *lipi*, the Kharoṣṭhī and the Bhaṭṭiprolu variety of the Brāhma alphabet is certain. The bearing of the early existence of such a list of alphabets and of the myth, ascribing their invention to Brahman, on the question of the antiquity of writing in India, is obvious. The introduction of writing cannot have taken place about 400 B. C., but must be earlier at least by some centuries.

Another passage of the Jaina Samavāyāṅga Sūtra makes it possible to show how the popular Brāhma alphabet looked about 300 B. C. The Samavāyāṅga includes a detailed abstract of the lost *Dṛṣṭivāda*, the twelfth of the Jaina Aṅgas, and asserts that according to this work, the *Bambhī livī* or Brāhma

---

[1] As stated above, I adhere to the tradition, which asserts that Pāṇini was the pupil of Upavarṣa and lived during the reign of the last Nanda, the predecessor of the Maurya Candragupta. This tradition gives a reasonable date and probably goes back itself to the beginning of our era, since, according to the concurrent testimony of Kṣemendra and Somadeva, it occurred in Guṇāḍhya's Bṛhatkathā. I agree with Dr. Burnell (El. S. Ind. Pal.[2], p. 6) and Professor A. Ludwig, (see his paper on "Yavanānī" quoted above) that *yavanānī* means "the writing of the Greeks". But I believe with Prof. Ludwig that Pāṇini's acquaintance with the existence of the Greek alphabet is by no means irreconcilable with his traditional date. Irrespective of the general reasons, adduced by Professor Ludwig, it seems to me not wonderful that an author, whose native country had been explored in 509 B. C. by Skylax and whose countrymen, the Gandhāras, had furnished a contingent for Xerxes' invasion of Greece should mention the old Oriental name of the Greeks and should be acquainted with their writing (see also Professor Weber, Monatsberichte Berl. Akad. 1871, p. 616). And there is, as Mr. Rapson points out to me, even positive proof for such an acquaintance, as Athenian *drakhmes* with the inscription ΑΘΕ struck before the end of the reign of Alexander, possibly even before 350 B. C., have been found in India as well as *Indian imitations* of such coins, see B. V. Head, Cat. Greek. Coins: Attica, p. XXXIf., pp. 25—27. To me it seems absolutely impossible to make the mere occurrence of the word Yavana in Sanskrit works a mark, which proves that they must have been written after the invasion of Alexander.

[27] alphabet consisted of 46 *māuyakkhara (mātṛkākṣara)* or radical signs.[1] The commentator Abhayadeva says that this number comes out by deducting from the (in his time, saec. XI) ordinary alphabet the vowels *ṛ, ṝ, ḷ, ḹ* and the lingual *ḷa,* but including *kṣa.* The reckoning is correct, as may be seen from a comparison of the oldest written alphabet, that on the Horiuzi palmleaf, which gives 51 signs, viz:—

a, ā, i, ī, u, ū, ṛ, ṝ, ḷ, ḹ (10), *e, ai, o, au, aṃ, aḥ, ka, kha, ga, gha* (20), *ṅa, ca, cha, ja, jha, ña, ṭa, ṭha, ḍa, ḍha* (30), *ṇa, ta, tha, da, dha, na, pa, pha, ba, bha* (40), *ma, ya, ra, la, va, śa, ṣa, sa, ha, ḷaṁ* (50), *kṣa.*[2]

If the four vowels and *ḷa* are deducted, only 46 radical signs remain. Nevertheless Abhayadeva's explanation undoubtedly contains a mistake. It is not the consonant *ḷa* but the group *kṣa,* which ought to be deducted. For *ḷa* is one of the ancient radical signs and occurs on the Sānchi Stūpa as well as in the Bhaṭṭiprolu alphabet. *Kṣa,* on the other hand, can have been reckoned as a radical sign only from the time, when *ka* was written with a loop or triangle on the left. It was only then that the origin of *kṣa*, in wich *ka* retained its ancient dagger-shape, was obscured and that the still prevalent erroneous conception of the indigenous schoolmasters could arise, who persistently declare *kṣa* to be a *mātṛkā.* The period, when the *ka* with a loop came into general use probably falls not earlier than between 400 and 500 A. D. In the inscriptions of the nail-headed and flat-topped (Nāgarī) types, it is only traceable since the second half of the sixth century. But in the ordinary literary characters it appeared earlier, as the Horiuzi palmleaf shows.

With respect to the omission of the vowels *ṛ, ṝ, ḷ, ḹ,* Abhayadeva is undoubtedly right, as they are missing in all the ancient and modern alphabets, used in the elementary Ind-

---

[1] See Weber, Indische Studien, vol. XVI, p. 281f. and Verzeichniss der Sanskrit und Prakrit Handschriften, vol. II, pt. II, p. 408, where better readings of the text are given.

[2] See Anecdota Oxoniensia, Aryan Series, vol. I, pt. 3, plates 1 and 2. The alphabet of the Cambridge MS. Add. No. 1049 has one letter less, as it omits *ḷa* which is unknown in Nepal and other parts of Northern India as in Kashmir.

[28] ian schools and by the classes without a scientific Brahminical education. According to the printed Lalitavistara, p. 145f., prince Siddhārtha explained on entering the writing-school to his master the hidden meaning of the radical signs of the alphabet which he was to learn.[1] The vowels, which he is said to have enumerated, are only twelve, viz:—*a, ā, i, ī, u, ū, e, ai, o, au, aṃ, aḥ*. These twelve vowels alone occur in the alphabet, taught in the indigenous Indian schools, where they are combined with the consonants and form the so-called *Bārākhaḍī* or *Bārasakhaḍī*,[2] which the children on beginning their school-course are made to copy incessantly, until by its means they have learned both elementary reading and writing. The *Bārākhaḍī*, in Sanskrit *dvādaśākṣarī*, "a collection or aggregate of twelve syllables (for each consonant)", is arranged as follows[3]:—

A Ā I Ī U Ū E AI O AU Aṃ Aḥ

1	*ka*	*kha*	*ga*	*gha*	*ṅa*	and so on through all the consonants.
2	*kā*	*khā*	*gā*	*ghā*	*ṅā*	
3	*ki*	*khi*	*gi*	*ghi*	*ṅi*	
4	*kī*	*khī*	*gī*	*ghī*	*ṅī*	
5	*ku*	*khu*	*gu*	*ghu*	*ṅu*	
6	*kū*	*khū*	*gū*	*ghū*	*ṅū*	
7	*ke*	*khe*	*ge*	*ghe*	*ṅe*	
8	*kai*	*khai*	*gai*	*ghai*	*ṅai*	
9	*ko*	*kho*	*go*	*gho*	*ṅo*	
10	*kau*	*khau*	*gau*	*ghau*	*ṅau*	
11	*kaṃ*	*khaṃ*	*gaṃ*	*ghaṃ*	*ṅaṃ*	
12	*kaḥ*	*khaḥ*	*gaḥ*	*ghaḥ*	*ṅaḥ*	

[1] This alphabet, too, included 46 mātṛkās. But the Calcutta edition omits, no doubt erroneously, among the consonants the dental *la*. The last letter is *kṣa*.

[2] The word is usually pronounced Bārā-khāḍī instead of Bārākhaḍī, because its etymology is no longer remembered.

[3] The Bārākhaḍī has been printed in Bombay and can be obtained through Pandit Jeshṭaram Mukundji. It is described by Molesworth, Marāṭhī Dictionary *sub voce* बारसकडी, and by Narmadāshankar in his Gujarātī Dictionary *sub voce* बाराखडी. This latter work states that the syllables *ka, kā* and so forth down to *kaḥ* are the Bārākhaḍī of *ka*.

[29] This *Bārākhaḍī*, which is used in all the parts of India known to me,[1] has of course always the same number of vowels, but the number of the consonants varies. In the Marāṭhā country and in Gujarāt, there are 36 instead of 34, the groups *kṣa* and *jña* being reckoned as simple radical signs and placed after *ḷa*. As usually a Maṅgala or invocation *oṃ namaḥ siddham* is prefixed to it, it is sometimes called by the Pandits the *Siddhamātṛkā* or *Siddhākṣarasamāmnāyaḥ* or "the alphabet, preceded by the word *Siddha* (success)", or jocularly *Mātṛkāpurāṇa* "the Purāṇa of the Mothers (radical signs)".

Its great antiquity is attested by the Chinese writers. Hiwen Tsiang states in the Siyuki[2] that the instruction of the young Hindus began with the practice in the twelve *chang* or tables. What these twelve tables were, appears from an account of the Indian alphabet and elementary instruction, given by Hui-lin[3] who wrote between A. D. 788—810. According to him the thirty four consonants, the last of which was *kṣa,* were each first combined with the twelve vowels *a—aḥ,* and thus a table or syllabary was formed identical with the modern Bārākhaḍī, which bore (according to another authority) the name Siddhavastu "the matter (preceded by the word) *siddha*". Next came ligatures of each consonant with *ya, ra, la, va, sa, ha* and the five nasals, and each of these ligatures was again combined with the twelve vowels. The result was a set of eleven further tables, which were, as the author says, in common use. Though Hui-lin calls these tables *fan* or "cycles",

---

[1] It is also used for the pagination of MSS. in Burma, Siam and Ceylon. In the former two countries the vowels are 12, in Ceylon 16, see the Grundriss, I, 11, p. 82 f.

[2] See, St. Julien, Mémoires etc., I, 72 and note, where, however, the translation has "un livre en douze sections" and the note alleges that the book was a syllabary, composed by Brahman and called Siddhavastu. In a letter to me, quoted in the first edition of this essay, Prof. J. Legge has pointed out that the Chinese text has nothing about "a book", but merely "12 *chang*" or tables.

[3] See Dr. A. von Rosthorn's letter to me in the WZKM (Vienna Oriental Journal) X, 280, the contents of which are summarised in the above account. My former conjecture that the expression "12 *chang*" is a translation of *dvādaśākṣarī* (Bārākhaḍī) and stands for "12 (syllable) table" is of course not tenable.

it is not doubtful, as Dr. A. von Rosthorn remarks, that they are identical with Hiwen Tsiang's twelve *chang*. It thus appears that the system of instruction in writing, described by Hui-lin and Hiwen Tsiang, is based on the Bārākhaḍī still used, but is further developed in accordance with the requirements of Sanskrit teaching. But the four vowels, *ṛ, ṝ, ḷ, ḹ* are not included, and Hui-lin, who mentions them expressly, states that ordinary people and beginners did not know them, as well as that they were employed as 'expletives' by grammarians. Hiwen Tsiang, too, excludes them from the ordinary alphabet which, as he says in the Siyuki, I, 77 (Beal), contained 47 letters i. e. the 12 vowels and 35 consonants, *ka—ha, ḷa* and *kṣa.*

[30] The omission of the four liquid vowels may also be inferred from the fragments of an alphabet of the Maurya period, originally discovered by Sir A. Cunningham at Mahābodhi Gayā[1] and lately re-examined by Dr. G. A. Grierson.[2] In the cloistered walk, which according to the tradition Aśoka erected over the supposed *Caṅkama* of Buddha, there is a double row of pillar bases,[3] eleven on each side, on which according to Dr. Grierson the following letters are still visible:

South

										A
•	•	•	•	•	•	•	•	•	•	•
11	10	9	8	7	6	5	4	3	2	1
				cha		*ṅa*				*ka*
•	•	•	•	•	•	•	•	•	•	•
22	21	20	19	18	17	16	15	14	13	12

North

The *A* on No. 1 is according to Dr. Grierson laid on its side, and the *ṅa* on No. 16 is in the same position. If the sign , which is here given according to a photographic quarter size reproduction of Dr. Grierson's photo-etching (Rep., Figure 3), is set up straight , we obtain a form closely agreeing with those

[1] Mahābodhi Gayā, p. 8f. Plates III and X, 1.

[2] Report to the Secr. Gov^t of Bengal, General Dep^t, Nov. 25, 1895.

[3] The pillar base No. 1 with the letter *A* has been transferred to the Aśoka Gallery of the Indian Museum at Calcutta, together with two others which at present bear no letters, Grierson, Report, p. 2.

in the Mathurā inscriptions of the Kushana period.[1] There is besides one pillar shaft, at present erroneously fixed in the base with *ka,* which, as Dr. Grierson's facsimile (loc. cit.) shows, bears a mutilated *A,* laid on its side. Sir A. Cunningham does not mention the *ṅa* on No. 16, but instead gives a round-topped *ga* on No. 13, as well as *ja* on No. 19 and *ṭa* on No. 22 as visible at the time of his visit (1881). Dr. Grierson however states that these signs are not to be traced at present. He also declares it to be improbable that the *ja* was actually seen by Sir A. Cunningham "as the fractures [on the spot where the letter ought to stand] are evidently very old", and he conjectures (Rep., p. 5) that Sir A. Cunningham's round-topped *ga* is "merely a faulty impression" of the sign on No. 16.[2]

However that may be, and even if the additional *ja* and *ṭa* mentioned by Sir A. Cunningham are left out of count, it is evident that the masons had numbered the pillar bases, and probably also the corresponding shafts, with the letters of the Brāhma alphabet arranged according to the phonetic principles of the grammarians and of the Bārākhaḍī. As the first base of the southern row is marked with the letter *A* and No. 12, the first of the northern row, with *ka,* it is further evident that the masons' alphabet included eleven vowel-signs, one less than the Bārākhaḍī. And it becomes also probable that among them were, as Sir A. Cunningham conjectured, the signs for Ā, I, Ī, U, Ū, E, AI, O, AU and that the last was either *Aṃ* or *Aḥ,*[3] one of them being inadvertently omitted. The liquid vowels cannot have had a place here, since they would make the total of the vowel signs sixteen and it would be necessary to assume that the masons skipped five of them.

---

[1] See the Grundriss, I, 11, Tafel III, 10, IV and especially 40, III. In the second Mathurā letter we have likewise the little knob on the left, caused by the scribe's making the bottom-stroke separately.

[2] On comparing Sir A. Cunningham's facsimiles, op. cit., Plate X, 1 with Dr. Grierson's, it seems to me evident that the former reproduce drawings or at least corrected impressions of rubbings.

[3] As Dr. Grierson has pointed out, there is no sufficient reason for declaring with Sir A. Cunningham that the last letter must have been *Aḥ.*

As the Indian masons are neither great scholars nor quite illiterate,[1] it may be assumed that the alphabet, which they used, is the popular one of the elementary schools of the day.

[31] The discovery of the Gayā alphabet possesses, as Sir A. Cunningham has pointed out, considerable importance for the history of Indian writing. As its fragments are arranged on phonetic principles and as they include the guttural *ṅa*, which never occurs in the old Prakrit inscriptions, it must have been framed for the requirements of Sanskrit. And it is at least highly probable that its formation is due to the Brahmans, whose influence and peculiar theories are also recognisable, as will appear further on, in the manner of the derivation of the secondary signs from the original ones. In the third century B. C., it appears, the state of things in the elementary schools was the same as in our days. The children learnt an alphabet which was not intended for their vernacular dialects, and this was no doubt due to the circumstance that already then (as later when the legend regarding Buddha's Brahminical writing-master Viśvāmitra arose, and also in modern times) the elementary instruction was chiefly in the hands of the Brahmans, who did not think it worth the while to alter for the sake of their Prakrit speaking pupils the alphabet, invented and suited for the peculiar *bhāṣā* of their schools and class.

Finally there are explicit statements in Chinese Buddhist works, discovered and kindly communicated to me by M. Sylvain Lévi, according to which the signs for the four liquid vowels were invented either by Nāgārjuna or by Śarvavarman, the minister of Ṣātavāhana. This tradition points at all events to the conclusion that even in later times the Hindus were aware of the fact that the ancient Brāhma alphabet contained only twelve vowel signs.

---

[1] The Indian masons, the *sūtradhāras* or *vardhakins* of the older literature and the *silețās* of our days, occupy an intermediate position between the Aryan and the Śūdra classes. They wore and still wear the sacred thread, and they possessed and still possess a small amount of Sanskrit learning. The rules of their craft, which they commit to memory, are written in Sanskrit, and are at present largely mixed with Prakrit and barbarous bastard forms.

If we return to the passage of the Samavāyāṅga Sūtra, the various facts adduced make it plain that Abhayadeva's explanation of the extract from the *Dṛṣṭivāda* is substantially correct. The forty-six radical signs of the ancient *Brāhmī lipi* included twelve vowels *a, ā, i, ī, u, ū, e, ai, o, au, aṃ, aḥ* and thirty four consonants viz, the twenty five of the five *Vargas*, the four liquids, the three sibilants, the spirant *ha* and in all probability not *kṣa*, but *ḷa*. It appears further, that there is no reason to distrust the Jaina tradition, according to which the statement of the *Dṛṣṭivāda* goes back at least to the reign [32] of the Maurya Candragupta, as his grandson's masons had learnt an alphabet, apparently agreeing with that described in the Jaina Aṅga in the most important particular.

The result of this enquiry, which shows that the popular Indian alphabet of the third century B. C. had no signs for the vowels *ṛ*, *ṝ*, *ḷ* and *ḹ*, will not surprise those who have paid attention to Indian palaeography. The long *ḹ*, the existence of which (as a sound) is denied by the grammarians of Pāṇini's school, is an invention probably due to the Brahminical *Kabbala*, the so-called Mantraśāstra, which seems to have been studied and used for charms by Brahmans, Buddhists and Jainas at least since the beginning of our era. The sign for the intial *Ḹ* occurs first on the Horiuzi palmleaf and in the ancient Cambridge MS. from Nepal, Add. No. 1049, where it consists of two cursive *la* interlaced (see Tafel VI of the Grundriss). Medial *ḹ* is, as far as I know, not traceable in any old document. Among the remaining three sounds, only the short *ṛ* occurs as an initial in words of the ordinary language, while initial *Ṝ* and *Ḷ* are used only in the technical terms of the Vyākaraṇa and other Śāstras. The ancient signs for the initial *Ḷ*, which again are found on the Horiuzi palmleaf and in the Cambridge MS. Add. No. 1049, are cursive forms of *la*. Medial *ḷ* is expressed in the inscriptions mostly by *li*. But in the Haidarabad grant of Pulikeśi II (Ind. Ant. vol. VI, 72, pl. II[a], l. 7), we find a cursive *la* in *kḷpta*, see also the Grundriss, I, 11, Tafel VII, 42. XIV and p. 65. A similar sign occurs also in the same word in Rudradeva's Annamkonda inscription, l. 118, see Ind. Ant. vol. XI, facs. at p. 14—15. The principles, on which the more common signs for initial and medial *ṛ*, *ṝ* have been framed, are (1) initial ṛ and ṝ are expressed by a *ra* with the signs for medial ṛ and ṝ, (2) medial ṛ is a modification of *ra*, produced either by a twist of the *ra*-stroke to the left with or without a curve to the right at the end, or by the addition of a curl at the end of the *ra*-stroke, (3) medial ṝ is invariably expressed by the double medial ṛ of the period. Thus we find for *vṛ* in the Northern inscriptions of the first and second centuries A. D. वृ or वृ and in the fourth century and later वृ, while the inscriptions and even the modern alphabets of the Southern type offer वृ. The northern initial Ṛ, which appears first in the Bower MSS.,[1] is ऋ *i. e. ra* with the curve of the medial ṛ attached, and [33] the southern forms of the letter, the oldest example of which occurs in a Kādamba grant of the fourth or fifth century,[2] appear to be modifications of the northern sign. These facts indicate that the signs for medial ṛ and ṝ were developed first and that those for the initials came into use somewhat later. As will be shown below, the process is exactly the reverse of that followed in the cases of the other vowels, where the medial signs are identical with, or modifications of, the initial ones. It is evident that the formation first of initial and next of medial vowels is the natural method, when an alphabet without vowel-signs is turned into one with vowels. Hence the palaeographic facts, too, show that the signs for ṛ and ṝ were not framed at the same time with those for *i, ī, u, ū, e, ai, o, au,* and that in all probability they are later inventions.

III.

If we now turn to the consideration of the oldest Indian inscriptions, it is not difficult to show that the palaeographic facts fully confirm the results, which the preceding examination of the ancient literature has yielded. They likewise show that writing, and especially the Brāhmī lipi, had had a long history in India, before king Piyadasi-Aśoka caused his Edicts to be incised in the various provinces of his large empire. In ad-

[1] Compare also for the several forms of ṛ and Ṛ the Grundriss, I, 11, Tafel III, 7, IX; 34, III; 37, VI; Tafel IV, 7, III; 39, III; Tafel VI, 18, IV; 43, III and Tafel VI, 7, I—II.

[2] Ind. Ant., vol. VI, p. 23, pl. III, l. 12.

dition they permit us to recognise that the Brāhmī lipi is the real old Indian alphabet, which was popularly used in the third century B. C. all over India, and that it was fully developed [34] before the introduction of the Kharoṣṭhī, whence we may infer that it is the writing which the Buddhist canonical works mention so frequently.

That the Brāhmī lipi was in the third century an ancient alphabet with a long history is proved by the very considerable variations in the forms of its signs found in the several versions of the Edicts, as well as by the recent discovery, on Sir A. Cunningham's Eraṇ coin, of a variety which runs from the right to the left, and of another one, on the Bhaṭṭiprolu relic caskets, which includes a number of more archaic forms and independent developments.

As regards Aśoka's Edicts, even a cursory inspection of good impressions or of trustworthy facsimiles, such as those of Drs. Burgess, Fleet and Hultzsch, reveals the existence of numerous differences in the formation of the several characters. A more careful study shows not only that almost every letter[1] has two, three, half a dozen or more sometimes widely divergent forms, but also that certain peculiarities are confined to particular districts, as well as that the great majority of the apparently or really more advanced forms, which appear more or less constantly in the inscriptions of the next three or four centuries, are found already in the Edicts. And it is significant that the local differences observable permit us to speak of a Northern and a Southern variety of the ordinary Brāhma alphabet, between which, as in later times, roughly reckoning, the river Narmadā marks, the boundary line.

In order to show, how considerable the divergences are, I give here the eight chief varieties of the initial *A*,[2] among which the first and the last show hardly any resemblance, though if all eight are placed side by side their connexion is easily recognised.

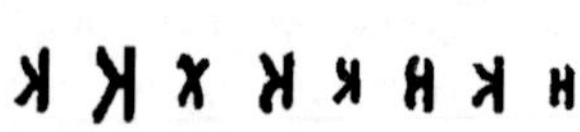

[1] According to Tafel II of my Grundriss der indischen Palaeographie the only exceptions are the letters *U, jha, ña, ṭa, ṭha, ṇa, tha* and *na*.

[2] The same varieties are of course found also in the initial *ā*.

It is not difficult to see, that the first seven varieties have been caused by two conflicting tendencies, a liking for [35] angles and a liking for curves, which are observable also in the divergent forms of other Brāhma letters. Nos 1—3 are purely angular. The first and the second differ only thereby, that in the one the obtuse angle touches the vertical line, and that in the other it has been first made separate and then connected by a short crossbar.[1] In the third form the right hand stroke is slightly bent in the middle and the whole letter resembles a Greek Xi. Nos 6 and 7 show on the left, instead of the straight sides of the angle, two well developed curves, and in No 6 they are united in the middle, while in No 7 they do not touch. Nos 4—5 appear to be mixed forms, as the former has on the left a curve below with a straight stroke slanting towards the left, while in the latter the curve stands above and the straight stroke below. This apparent mixture may be due to an incomplete change of the older, angular form. But the two varieties may also be explained as cursive developments from No 6, the writer not caring to make the more elaborate curve twice. No 8, finally, is a purely cursive development from No 6, a straight stroke being substituted for the notched line on the left.

Now the local distribution of these forms, which with the exception of Nos 2 and 3 are of very frequent occurrence, is as follows. The angular forms Nos 1—3, as well as the variety mentioned in note 1, are confined to the Southern versions of the Edicts. They appear only in Girnār and Siddāpur, Dhauli and Jaugada, and it may be noted that in Girnār and Siddāpur they are in the majority, Nos 4—7 appearing only occasionally, while in the two Southeastern versions (with the exception of the Jaugada Separate Edicts) the contrary is the case. On the other hand I know of no case where a purely angular form is found in the Kālsī, Delhi, Bairāt, Sanchi, Allahābād, Mathia, Radhia, Rampūrva Barābar, Sahasrām and Rūpnāth Edicts. In the majority of these documents Nos 4—7 alone are used. No 8 occurs very frequently in Kālsī (some-

---

[1] There are also instances in which this crossbar is omitted and the angle stands by itself, see *e. g. amisā*, Siddāpur I, l. 3.

times with small variations) and once or twice in Râmpûrva. Hence it would appear that the angular forms are southern [36] peculiarities and that, as they are undoubtedly the more ancient ones, they furnish an instance of the conservatism, frequently observable in the southern alphabets of later times. This inference is confirmed by the fact that other ancient inscriptions of the same or nearly the same period, like those on the Kolhapur and Bhaṭṭiprolu relic caskets and from the Nānāghāt cave, likewise show the angular forms, (mostly side by side with the curved ones), while the documents, found north of the Narmadā, such as those on the Bharahut and Sānchi Stūpas and in the Nāgārjunī caves, as well as the coins of Agathocles offer almost exclusively the *A* with two curves, rarely the mixed form No 4. A solitary exception in Mahābodhi Gayā (Cunningham, op. cit., plate V, No 2) may be explained by the consideration that, as the dialect of several Gayā inscriptions shows, Southerners came to visit that famous place of pilgrimage, and that the person who wrote the copy may have been a Southron.

In addition to the local differences in the form of the initial *A* and *Ā*, there are also others observable in *kha, ja, ma, ra* and *sa,* which may be briefly noticed here, though the full details must be reserved for the discussion of the palaeography of the Edicts in my *Grundriss.*[1] The *kha* with a circle[2] or loop at the foot, a very ancient form, alone is used in Kālsī and besides occurs only in Jaugada together with the simplified forms showing a dot instead of the circle or no appendage at all. The *ja* with a loop in the middle[3] is used only in Kālsī. It seems to be a form peculiar to the extreme North and the Northwest, as it is found also on the coins of Agathocles and of the Taxila merchants (see below p. 48 f.). The other northern versions have mostly a secondary development from it, the *ja* with a dot in the middle (plate I, No 7, Col. V, c) more rarely the independent form (given under No 7, Col. V, d), which is used exclusively in Girnār together with its derivative,

[1] See now the Grundriss der Indo-Ar. Phil. und Alt. I, 11, p. 34ff.

[2] See plate I of this paper, No. 19, Col. V, a.

[3] See plate I, No. 7, Col. V, b.

the later angular *ja* with three horizontal bars (see below p. 41). The *ma* with the angle at the top, an ancient form, (plate I, No 13, Col. V) occurs in the southern versions (with the exception of Siddāpur), where an open square appears instead of the angle) [37] and is used exclusively in Girnār. All the northern versions of the Edicts have a semicircle instead of the angle. The angular and wavy forms of *ra* and their insertion in the verticals of consonants are also peculiar to the southern versions (Girnār and Siddāpur); the solitary *ra* in the Rūpnāth Edict consists of an almost straight stroke. Finally, the ancient *sa* with a straight limb on the left (plate I, No 15, Col. VI, b) is likewise confined to the South (Girnār and Siddāpur).

These facts, to which some more might be added, are sufficient to show, that the very common idea[1] of the homogeneousness of the characters of the Edicts and of the absence of local varieties, is erroneous. The differences between the writing of the northern and the southern versions are quite as considerable as those, found four hundred forty years later, between the letters of the northern and southern inscriptions of the first and second centuries A. D.[2] And it must be kept in mind that the circumstances, under which the Edicts were engraved, were not favourable to a full expression of the local varieties of the letters. Copies were sent out from Pāṭaliputra into the provinces, which were recopied and, as the dialectic differences in the language and occasional peculiarities in the wording prove, also recast by the clerks of the district-governors, before they were made over for engraving to the masons. It seems only natural to

---

[1] See *e. g.* Burnell, El. South Indian Palaeography, p. 7, note 4, with whose remarks Dr. Taylor, M. Halévy and others agree.

[2] I state this in accordance with the facts, shown by Tafel III of my Grundriss, which includes *inter alia* the signs from the inscriptions of the Śakas and Kuṣanas of Mathurā, Kāman and Sānchi, the Western Kṣatrapas, the Andhras and Ābhīras. Dr. Burnell's statement (loc. cit.) that "in the course of a few hundred years [after Aśoka] the alphabets used in Gujarat and Bengal had already become so different as to be very little alike in appearance", I fear, cannot be substantiated. Between 200 B. C. and 200 A. D. there are no inscriptions from Bengal proper. The inscriptions from Mahābodhi Gayā in Behar (given by Sir A. Cunningham) which may be assigned to this period, look very much like those of the Śakas and the Western Kṣatrapas.

assume that the characters of the copies prepared at Pāṭaliputra influenced the writing of the provincial clerks, and caused the introduction of forms, otherwise not usual in the several [38] provinces.[1] Such a suspicion is the more natural, as the provincial clerks have in no case completely changed the language, but have always allowed some Māgadhisms to stand. But, however that may be, local differences are traceable in the writing of the several versions and they prove that the Brāhma alphabet had had a long history before the third century B. C. If the slowness of the change of the forms, and the comparative insignificance of the local variations which the inscriptions of the next four or five centuries show, are taken as the standard, it will be necessary to assume that the letters of the Edicts had been used at least during four or five hundred years.

As regards the second important point, to which attention has been called above, viz., the occurrence of numerous apparently or really advanced forms, identical or closely agreeing

[1] As I have stated already in Dr. Burgess' Arch. Surv. Rep. W. I., Vol. IV, p. 79 f. and in the Ind. Ant., Vol. XII, 190, the clerks who prepared the fair copies of the inscriptions, not the masons or coppersmiths who engraved them, are the men who influenced the formation of the letters. How the masons worked, may be seen from two passages of the Kālsī version. In the twelfth Edict, l. 31 six letters have been scored out and the corrections have been written above the line. The letters in the upper row are as large as those in the lower and the distance between lines 30 and 31 becomes from the beginning of the corrected passage twice as great as it was before. It is evident that the mistake and its correction occurred in the MS. given to the mason. If they were due to the latter, the line would run on straighter and the letters of the correction would be smaller. Again in the fourteenth Edict l. 20 the syllables *ṭite* of the word *ghaṭite* are corrections, one standing above the line and the other below it. But the distance between *gha* and the first letter of the following word, *ma,* is twice as great as those intervening between the other letters of the line. Here it is again certain that the MS. had the mistake and the correction. If the mason had skipped the two signs and added them afterwards, the *gha* would not stand further off from *ma* than from its predecessor. I think that these two instances are sufficient to prove that Aśoka's masons copied quite mechanically. It seems, therefore, impossible to attribute to them any other influence on the shape of the letters than such as may be caused by a slip of the chisel or by their accidentally overlooking a stroke in the MS. before them.

with those of the later times, its significance will become best apparent, if all such signs, found in the Edicts, are placed together. The subjoined little table, for the preparation of which [39] I have to acknowledge the help of Dr. W. Cartellieri, gives in the lines, marked *A*, the advanced Aśoka letters photolithographed according to cuttings from the facsimiles, and in those, marked *B*, the corresponding characters from the later inscriptions of Hathigumphā, the Nānāghāt, Mathurā and the Western caves. The dates of the latter vary between the middle of the second century B. C. and of the second century A. D., and in every case the oldest available counterpart has been chosen.

The table shows that the later signs for sixteen letters occur already in the third century B. C. Four of these forms, the dagger-shaped *ka* (common in Kālsī and occurring in most other versions except in Girnār), the angular *gha* (Kālsī) and *ha* (No 21, in various versions) as well as the curved *ḍa* (Kālsī) are in reality archaic,[1] while the corresponding common signs of the Edicts are advanced developments, which like the peculiar *va* (No 18, Girnār, Sohgaurā), and *sa* (No 20, Kālsī, Jaugada), have left no trace in the later writing. The remaining ones are really cursive or derived from cursive forms. No 1, the initial *A*, has been discussed above, its counterpart in line *B*

[1] See below pp. 58f., 61, 73. The counterparts in line *B* are from the Hathigumphā inscription.

occurs in the Kuṣana inscriptions from Mathurā. No 3, the *kha* with a loop to the right (Kālsī) is a cursive form for the *kha* with the circle at the foot,[1] and itself the parent of No 4 [40] (Delhi-Sivalik) which preserves the twist in the down stroke caused by the loop, but substitutes a dot for the latter.[2] No 5, the *kha* with the triangle (once in Mathia) is a fanciful variant for the oldest form, its counterpart has been taken from the archaic Mathurā inscriptions. No 6, the *ga* with the round top[3] is a cursive form of the pointed letter, the corresponding form is from Hathigumphā, but found in all inscriptions of the second century B. C. No 8, the *cha* with two loops[4] is a tertiary development, immediately derived from the form with the bisected circle, which again is merely cursive.[5] The same remark applies to No 9, the *ja* with three bars. It is derived from the notched Girnār form, which itself is a cursive development from the Bhaṭṭiprolu form.[6] Nos 11 and 19, the stunted *ti* and *vi*[7], give examples of the triangulation of the lower portion of *va* and of the reduction of the vertical strokes so characteristic of the alphabets of the next centuries, which appears already with great regularity in the Nāgārjunī cave inscriptions of Aśoka's grandson. No 12, the

---

[1] See below plate I, No 19, Col. V, I.

[2] The corresponding forms in line *B* have been taken from Hathigumphā. Better ones for No 3 are found in the inscriptions from the Western caves, see Tafel III, 8, VIII of the Grundriss.

[3] Once in Delhi Sivalik Ed. VII and in the mason's alphabet at Mahābodhi Gayā.

[4] Kālsī once and mason's alphabet from Mahābodhi Gayā. The form in line *B* is from Hathigumphā.

[5] See below p. 68.

[6] See below plate I, No 7, Col. V, a and the discussion on No 7, p. 60f., The sign, given above, occurs in Girnār, Ed. IX, l. 1. The great length of the central bar is caused by the *ā*-stroke which it includes. Similar forms occur in Kālsī, where they represent the looped *ja*. The corresponding form in line *B* occurs already in Daśaratha's Nāgārjunī inscription.

[7] The stunted *ta* is very frequent in Kālsī and occurs occasionally also in other versions. The triangular *va* with the very short vertical is found once in a correction in Kālsī, Edict XIII, 2, l. 13. The forms in line *B* have been taken from the Kuṣana inscriptions. Some instances of *pa*, *pha* and *sa* with very short verticals occur likewise already in the Edicts.

da with a shallow curve and the tail twisted towards the right (Jaugada, Girnār, etc.) is a transitional form, corresponding to those in the Nāgārjunī cave, the archaic Mathurā and the Pabhosa inscriptions (*B*), and leading up to the *da* of the first [41] and second centuries A. D. Nos 13, 14 and 16 give examples of the introduction of angles in the lower limb of *pa, pha* and *la*,[1] which originally consisted of curves, but are changed with perfect regularity already in the Hathigumphā, the archaic Mathurā and the Pabhosa inscriptions.[2] No 15, the *bha* with the round side-limb (Jaugada, Kālsī, etc.) is of course cursive and found in all the later inscriptions except in Hathigumphā. Nos 17 and 22, the *la* and *ha* with the side-limbs turned downwards (Jaugada Separate Edicts) are again highly cursive. Counterparts of No 17 are found in the Nānāghāt inscription, those of No 22 only in the Ābhīra inscription from the Nāsik caves. These facts, to which others, such as later forms of the medial vowels, the position of the Anusvāra at the top of the consonants and the occasional use of *serifs* or short bars at the top of verticals, might be added, do not agree with the assumption that writing was a recent practice in Aśoka's times. To me it seems that they are most easily explained, on the supposition that several, both archaic and more advanced, alphabets existed in the third century B. C., that an archaic alphabet was chosen for the perpetuation of the Edicts, but that the clerks mixed the forms. And in support of this view I would adduce the Jaina tradition, discussed above p. 23 ff., according to which many alphabets were used about 300 B. C. But, even if we leave aside all conjectural explanations of the facts, it remains undeniable that the writing of the Edicts is in a state of transition, and this alone is sufficient to warrant the assertion, that their alphabet certainly had had a long history.[3]

---

[1] Nos 13 and 14 occur a few times in Kālsī and other versions, No 16 is from Delhi-Sivalik and occurs also in Kālsī, etc.

[2] Among the inscriptions of the second century B. C., that from the Nānāghāt cave preserves the round forms.

[3] As so distinguished an epigraphist as Dr. Burnell has come to exactly the contrary conclusion and as his view is still quoted by other writers on the subject, it will not be superfluous, if I briefly review his arguments. His chief argument for the late introduction of writing is that

[42] To an earlier stage than the writing of the Edicts belongs the inscription on Sir A. Cunningham's Eraṇ coin, which runs

---

very few allusions to the use of letters are contained in the literary works which date from the fourth century B. C. The answer to this statement is contained in the second part of this paper, and it need only be pointed out that Dr. Burnell could not know of the passages mentioning private and official documents, as the works, in which they occur, had not been published in 1878. His second and accessory argument is drawn from internal evidence furnished by the Edicts. He says, El. South Indian Palaeography, p. 2, "The inscriptions of Aśoka are also in themselves proofs that writing was about 250 B. C. a recent practice; for they present irregularities of every kind," and in the note to the passage, he quotes as instances, conflicting spellings like *añapitaṃ* (correctly *āñapitaṃ*) and *āñāpitaṃ, dasana* and *dasaṇa* (from the Girnār version), the irregular insertion of nasals before consonants (which, as he admits, may be due to the negligence of the masons) and the constant neglect of the reduplication of consonants *e. g.* in *piyasa* for *piyassa*, *ārabhisante* (read *ārabhisare*) for *ārabbhissare* and so forth. These facts are indisputable, and other similar ones like the irregular employment of the signs for sibilants in Kālsī, Bairāt II and Siddāpur and the constant or nearly constant use of short *i* and *u* for long *ī* and *ū* in Kālsī, Bairāt and Rūpnāth may be added. But they do not prove the proposition, in support of which Dr. Burnell adduces them. The numerous double and even treble forms of the same words, which occur in one and the same version are not graphic. Some are, as the analogies in the ancient literary Prakrits show, real variants which occurred in one and the same dialect, and some are due to slips in the translation of the Māgadhī originals of the Edicts into the Western and Northwestern dialects. The irregular use of the Anusvāra before consonants may also be ascribed partly to the same cause, since the Pali too occasionally omits a nasal and then doubles the following consonant. In other cases it may be due to the carelessness of Aśoka's clerks, who treated their Vernaculars exactly as a modern Karkun treats his. Everybody who has had any experience of Indian office work, must know that the *Sheras* or official papers, prepared by the clerks of the older generation, who had received their elementary instruction in the indigenous schools and had afterwards been trained in the offices, show an extreme irregularity in the use of the Anusvāras, of the short and long *i* and *u*, of the three signs for sibilants and of the reduplication of consonants. During my service as Educational Inspector I have seen a great many, sometimes important, documents from British Government offices and from those of native princes, which in their spelling were quite as bad as, and even worse than, Aśoka's Edicts, and I do not recollect that any papers, except those sent by carefully trained schoolmasters, were quite exact. One cause of this state of things was the wretched instruction in the indigenous schools,

[43] from the right to the left.[1] The letters agree exactly with Aśoka's and the *dha* has the position required for the writing from the left to the right. It dates, therefore, from a period during which the Brāhma characters were written in both directions. This period is probably not very far distant from the middle of the third century B. C., as the Edicts still show single letters, which belong to the writing from the right to the left, viz., the *dha,* given in the first Comparative Table No 4, Col. V, a, the *O,* ibidem, No 6, Col. VI, f, and the *ta,* ibidem, No 22, Col. V, l. The coin may, therefore, be somewhat younger than Sir A. Cunningham thinks, who assigns it to 400 B. C. The great antiquity of its find-spot, the town of Eraṇ, is attested by an inscription on the Sānchi Stūpa, where it occurs as *Erakina.*

A still more important palaeographic witness for the antiquity of the Brāhma alphabet is the variety, found in the inscriptions on the Bhaṭṭiprolu relic caskets, the value of which, I am sorry to say, I have somewhat underestimated in the in-

---

where writing is taught according to the Bārākhaḍī, described above, which contains no ligatures and more sibilants than the Vernaculars possess, and where composition received little or no attention, being at the best confined to the copying of a few forms for letters. Another cause was the want of a settled system for the minutiae of vernacular grammar, both in writing and in speech (compare my remarks, Ep. Ind., Vol. III, p. 136) all efforts in this direction being of quite recent date. A third cause is, I fear, the deeply rooted tendency of all Hindus to inaccuracy in small matters. Now the Aśoka Edicts are official papers, written by his *lipikaras* or clerks. As there is no reason for assuming that they had received a better education than the men in the modern offices of British and native India, and that the Vernaculars of the third century B. C. had been polished and perfected by grammarians, it seems difficult to ascribe the defects in their spelling to other causes than those which produce the same imperfections in the office work of the modern Karkuns. The probability that the causes are the same increases, if it is remembered, that even the Sanskrit landgrants, issued from the secretariats of later kings, show the same mistakes, sometimes in a very high degree. Thus the Valabhī grant, published in the Indian Antiquary, Vol. VII, p. 68 f., has no long ī, very few long ū, invariably *dha* for *ddha* and almost regularly *śa* for *ṣa.*

[1] Coins of Ancient India, p. 101 and plate XI, 18. According to a plaster cast, which I owe to the kindness of Mr. Rapson, the inscription is *Dhamapālasa.o,* the last consonant being illegible.

troductory remarks to my edition in the Epigraphia Indica, Vol. II, p. 323 ff. Though the article has been published only in 1894, it was written more than two years earlier, before I had begun to study the question of the derivation of the Brāhma [44] alphabet. Then, I saw only that the inscriptions probably belong to nearly the same period as the Edicts and that their alphabet, which offers the six independent Mātṛkās *gh, j, m, l, ṣ* and *ḷ* and the curious notation of *a* and *ā*, as well as some minor differences in the radical signs for *c, d* and *bh,* must be considered as coeval with Aśoka's Brāhma letters. Hence I drew the inference that in the third century the Brāhma characters showed in certain districts even greater local varieties than appears from the Edicts alone, and I pointed out that this discovery greatly bettered the position of those who, like myself, hold the art of writing to have been practised for many centuries before the times of the great Maurya reformer. So far I have nothing to change or to add.

But the comparison of the Indian characters with Semitic signs, which I have instituted since, has greatly altered my opinion regarding the palaeographic value of the independent signs. I no longer believe in the possibility to regard the *gha* of the Edicts as a derivative from *ga,* and admit now that the Bhaṭṭiprolu *gh* (below plate I, No 3, Col. VI) is an independent form, the framer or framers of the alphabet having discarded one of the old Semitic radicals, which the common Brāhma alphabet retains. I further must admit that the Bhaṭṭiprolu *j* (below plate I, No 7, Col. V, a) and *ṣ* (plate I, No 15, Col. V) are older forms than the corresponding ones of the Edicts, the former being a tolerably faithful representation of the oldest form of *Zain* and the latter being a simplification of the Semitic *Samech,* turned topsy-turry. The *l* and *ḷ* (below plate I, No 12, Col. V, 2, Col. VI), regarding which I did not say anything definite, I must now declare to be independent evolutions from the ancient Semitic *Lamed,* and even in the tailed *c* (below plate I, No 18, Col. V, 3) I now recognise an archaic form. On the other hand, for *m* ୡ, which I took to be a possibly older form of the ordinary Brāhma sign, I can no longer claim this distinction. It is merely the oldest *ma* of the Edicts, placed top downwards. This change of opinion regarding the details, the necessity for which will become more fully apparent in the next part of this paper, naturally forces me to modify the general proposition that the Bhaṭṭiprolu alphabet does not teach us much regarding the history of the Brāhma [45] writing and regarding the conversion of the Semitic letters into Indian characters. It certainly furnishes us with valuable intermediate forms for four radical signs, *c*, *j*, *l* and *ṣ*, which latter appears to be the parent of the ordinary Brāhma *ṣa* and *sa*, and with one entirely independent derivative sign *gh*. Its separation from the ordinary Brāhma alphabet must fall not only before the third century B. C., but also before the time, when the Eraṇ coin was struck, and cannot have happened at a later period than the fifth century B. C., though it may fall much earlier.

This estimate carries us back to the period, for which the passages of the Jātakas, the Pācittiya and the Mahāvagga, quoted above, assert the common use of writing, though they do not give the name of the characters employed nor any details regarding them, by which they might be identified. The coincidence makes it of course tempting to assume that the writing, referred to in the Buddhist Canon, is the Brāhmī lipi. And the correctness, or at least the great probability of this assumption, I think, is made apparent by the recent discoveries regarding the relative position of the Brāhmī and the Kharoṣṭhī — the only other script which could come into question — as well as by the facts bearing on the origin of the Kharoṣṭhī.

The late finds of very ancient inscribed coins in Northwestern India leave no doubt that according to the epigraphic evidence the Brāhmī lipi was since the beginning of the historical period the paramount Indian alphabet, used from the Himalayas to Cape Komorin and from the Khyber Pass to the Bay of Bengal, while the Kharoṣṭhī held always a secondary place only in a very confined territory. Again, the clear evidence of the forms of the Kharoṣṭhī letters, the original stock of which is doubtlessly derived from the Aramaic alphabet of 500—400 B. C., shows that this alphabet cannot have been developed, much less have penetrated into Eastern India at the early period to which the Buddhist works refer.

The first point, which is of considerable general importance for Indian palaeography, will best become intelligible by a brief review of the epigraphy of those districts where Kharoṣṭhī inscriptions occur. From the third century we have the two Kharoṣṭhī versions of the Aśoka Edicts, incised in the [46] northwestern corner of the Panjab, at Shāhbāzgarhī and Mansehra. To the same or possibly a somewhat earlier period belong Sir A. Cunningham's coins from the site of the Taxila or Takṣaśilā, which prove the contemporaneous popular use of the Brahma characters in Gandhāra.

These coins have been figured by Sir A. Cunningham in his Coins of Ancient India, plates II and III. He has pointed out, op. cit. p. 61, that they are partly punch-marked silver pieces and partly single or double die copper pieces, all of the standard peculiar to India, and he takes them for this reason and on account of the very archaic forms of the letters of the legends, "to be anterior to the Greek conquest of Alexander". It will perhaps be safer to say "anterior to the Greek conquest of Demetrius". From their inscriptions, which are partly in Brāhma characters of the Kālsī type[1] and partly both in Brāhma and in Karoṣṭhī letters, Sir A. Cunningham has already drawn the obvious inference, that both alphabets were used in Northern India during the third century B. C. Something more, it seems to me, may be elicited from an analysis of the legends.

On the coin, plate II, 17, the Brāhma legend *Vaṭasvaka* corresponds to Sanskrit *Vaṭāśvakāḥ* and probably means "the Vaṭa-Aśvakas" or "the Aśvakas of the Vaṭa or 'fig-tree' division". It is well known that there was an Aśvaka tribe in Northwestern India, whom the Greeks call Assakenoi and state (Arrian, Indica, I. 1) to have inhabited the country west of the Indus as far as the Kophen. It may further be mentioned that some old Indian tribes, like the Yaudheyas[2] were actually divided into sections or *gaṇas,* as well as that, as the case of the Audumbaras shows, tribes were occasionally named after

---

[1] The Kālsī type is visible in the looped *ja.*

[2] See, Sir A. Cunningham, Arch. Surv. Reports, Vol. XIV, p. 141 and plate XXXI, where coins of their second and third *gaṇas* are described.

trees. With this explanation the coin appears to have been issued by one of the subdivisions of a tribe, which occupied just those districts, from which so many Kharoṣṭhī inscriptions come, and a Brāhma inscription on a tribal coin would certainly indicate that the alphabet was in popular use.

[47] The latter point comes out still more strongly through some other coins, figured on plate III,[1] viz.

Obverse	Reverse
No 9 *Dujaka* (Kharoṣṭhī)	*Negamā* (Brāhmī)
No 10 *Dojaka* (Brāhmī)	*Negamā* (Brāhmī)
No 8 *[T]ālima[ta]* (Brāhmī)	*[N]ega[m.]* (Brāhmī)
No 11 *A[taka?]takā* (Brāhmī)	*Negam[ā]* (Brāhmī)

The word *negamā* is common enough in Pali and in the epigraphic Prakrits, and means always 'the traders'. It shows here that the coins are mercantile money-tokens, issued by traders, and the words on the obverse may be either names of towns or of guilds.[2] The latter explanation is perhaps the more probable one. But however that may be, the use of both alphabets by traders proves indeed that both were in popular use in the heart of Gandhāra.

The other coins of the same period, struck outside the Panjab, show legends in Brāhmī, even that from Mathurā, op. cit. plate VIII, 1, in which town also a votive inscription in Brāhma characters of the third century (Reports Arch. Survey, Vol. XX, plate VI) has been found. Only in one case Kharoṣṭhī letters have turned up further south, but under circumstances, which do not allow the inference that the alpha-

[1] Though the letters are perfectly distinct, Sir A. Cunningham gives erroneously *Nekama* as the reading of the Kharoṣṭhī legend of No 9. On the obverse of No 8 he reads *Rālimata*, and he takes *negamā* as the equivalent of the Greek Νόμισμα, for which explanation there is no authority (see also Ind. Ant., vol. XXI, p. 346). He correctly points out that, on plate II, Nos 21 & 22 have the inscription *Kāḍasa*, i. e. *Kālasa*, in Brāhma letters of the type of the Edicts, and asserts that No 13 on plate III bears the Kharoṣṭhī legend *Pamca Nekamma*. According to the autotype the third sign is not *ne* but *a* and the fourth looks like *kra*.

[2] I am unable to explain *Dujaka-Dojaka*. *Tālimata* seems to be connected with the Sanskrit *Tālī* "Corypha Taliera" or "Flacourtia cataphracta".

bet was generally used or known. This case occurs in the Siddāpur Edicts where the writer Paḍa has added at the end his qualification *lipikareṇa* 'the scribe' in Kharoṣṭhī characters. This looks like a joke or a boast, as if Paḍa, proud of his accomplishments, had been anxious to make it apparent that he knew more than the ordinary characters. And, as he was [48] in the royal service, it is not unlikely that he may have acquired a knowledge of the Kharoṣṭhī during a stay in a northern office, or may have been a Northerner by birth.[1]

From the second and first centuries B. C. we have chiefly legends on coins, which were struck in the Panjab or in non-Indian countries further west. The Indo-Grecian kings generally use Kharoṣṭhī letters, but Agathokles and Pantaleon employ also Brāhma characters, showing thereby that this alphabet likewise continued to be used in the Northwest, side by side with the Kharoṣṭhī. The same fact is proved by the double legends in Kharoṣṭhī and Brāhma letters on Sir A. Cunningham's Audumbara and Kuninda coins, op. cit. pl. IV[2] and V, 1—6, which come from the same districts and probably belong to the same time. Further east in Kosambī, Ayodhyā (op. cit., pl. V, 7—18 and IX) and Pancāla (pl. VII) as well as further south in Ujjain (pl. X) none but Brāhma letters occur. And it is curious that even the Yaudheyas (pl. VI), who were settled on the lower Satledge, use only the latter characters. A few single letters on the gateway of the Bharahut Stūpa, among which there is a *sa* of the second century, (Cunningham, the Stūpa of Bharahut, pl. VIII), are probably marks of northern masons, who erected this additional portion of the monument for Dhanabhūti.

During the period of the Śaka and Kuṣana kings, from the first century B. C. to the end of the second century A. D.,

---

[1] See the Wiener Zeitschrift f. d. Kunde d. Morgenlandes, Vol. VII, p. 30f. Dr. Grierson, Ind. Ant., Vol. XXIV, p. 247, points out an analogous practice of the modern Kāyasths of Bihār who sign the documents, written in the Kaithī character, with their names in Arabic letters.

[2] The *Vṛṣṇi*-coin No 15 is according to the evidence of the characters later and probably belongs to the period when the Śakas had carried the Kharoṣṭhī as far as Mathurā. A few votive inscriptions of the second and first centuries B. C. from the same town are in Brāhma characters, Epigraphia Indica, Vol. II, p. 195.

the numerous inscriptions, incised in the Western Panjab, are in Kharoṣṭhī and those on Dr. Bhagvānlāl's Lion Capital prove that the Kharoṣṭhī penetrated during the reign of the Śaka Satrap and king Śuḍasa or Śoḍāsa as far as Mathurā, where however, as the enormous quantity of Jaina and Bauddha votive inscriptions shows, the Brāhma alphabet was at that time and later the usual one. [49] The coins of the earlier Śaka kings from the North like those of Mauos and Azes and of their Satraps, as well as those of Gondopherres and his brothers, have Greek and Kharoṣṭhī legends, while the later Kuṣana kings, Kaniṣka, Huviṣka and Bazodeo or Vāsudeva discard the latter, and their successors finally adopt the Brāhma alphabet. Further east and south the king and Satrap Rājubula and his son Śuḍasa, who ruled over Mathurā and perhaps over other portions of the eastern Panjab, either follow the same practice as Mauos or use Brāhma letters (Cunningham, op. cit., pl. VIII, 2—5), which occur also on the coins of the Satraps Hagamāsha and Hagamāna (ibidem, Nos 6—7). Further two foreign (Śaka?) Satraps and kings of Ujjain, Nahapāna and Caṣṭana employ on their coins both the Indian Alphabets simultaneously, while the inscriptions of Ayama, the minister of Nahapāna, of his daughter Dakṣamitrā and his son-in-law, the Śaka Uṣavadāta or Usabhadāta, as well as of the immediate descendants of Caṣṭana show exclusively Brāhma characters.

The epigraphic evidence shows therefore that in the third century the popular use of the Kharoṣṭhī was strictly confined to the Panjāb and that it was nothing more than a secondary script, running along by the side of the Brāhmī, which prevailed all over India. This state of things continued during the next two centuries. During the period of the Śaka rule the Kharoṣṭhī spread further south, without however losing its character as an accessory alphabet. A very strong argument for the assumption that its position was the same even in the fourth century B. C. is furnished by Mr. Rapson's discovery of Persian Sigloi with countermarks in Brāhma and Kharoṣṭhī letters (Jour. Roy. As. Soc., 1895, p. 865 ff.). For this reason and because the general prevalence of the Brāhma alphabet has now become more clearly apparent, it seems very probable that the Buddhist Canon can only refer to the latter.

The second point, the improbability that the Kharoṣṭhī was already developed or in general use even in its home as early as say 500 B. C. requires here only a few remarks as the details have been discussed fully below in Appendix I. Its derivation from the Aramaic alphabet has been generally accepted, ever since Mr. E. Thomas pointed it out, and the shape of its *ba, na, ra* and *va* makes a doubt impossible. According to Dr. I. Taylor's suggestion, The Alphabet, Vol. II, p. 261, which [50] is most probable on historical and palaeographical grounds, its immediate source is the Aramaic alphabet of the Akhaemenian period, and the introduction of the Aramaic letters into India dates from the time, when the Akhaemenian kings of Persia had conquered the Panjab, just those districts where the Kharoṣṭhī has its real home.[1] As the Persian con-

[1] M. Halévy, op. cit., p. 250ff. and particularly p. 267, tries to establish a still later date for the elaboration of the Kharoṣṭhī. He seeks the prototypes of its characters in the Aramaic alphabet of the fourth century B. C. He believes that they were developed in Ariana not earlier than 330 B. C. after the appointment of Macedonian Satraps by Alexander, who, as he thinks, may have fostered the use of the already prevalent Aramaic writing and thereby may have induced their subjects to adapt it to their special wants. The obvious weakness of M. Halévy's arguments prevents my accepting his theory, which would be more favourable for my point.

It is a matter of course that I am likewise unable to agree with M. Halévy's theory (op. cit., p. 280—286 and Plate II, A) according to which the Brāhmī lipi has borrowed from the Kharoṣṭhī six radical signs, *śa, jha, ḍa, ña, u* and *ra*, the Anunāsika, the system of vowel-notation, and the numeral signs 4—9. The reasons, why I do not consider the six Mātṛkās and the vowel-notation of the Brāhma alphabet as loans from the Kharoṣṭhī, will become apparent in the next section of this Essay. With respect to the Anunāsika, I must point out that the sign ँ, which M. Halévy derives from the Kharoṣṭhī *ma* 𐨨 of the Indo-Grecian coins, appears in no Indian document written in India before 1200 A. D., while the Kharoṣṭhī went out of use about 200 A. D. As regards the assertion that the Brāhma numeral signs for 4—9 are the initial Kharoṣṭhī letters for the words *catur, pañcan, ṣaṭ* (old Prakrit, *sa, chha* or *saḍ*), *saptan* (Prakrit *satta*), *aṣṭan* (old Prakrit *asta, aṭṭha*) and *navan* (old Prakrit *ṇava*), which is also put forward by Dr. Taylor (The Alphabet, II, p. 266), it is unfortunate that in four cases the facts are absolutely against it. The Kharoṣṭhī *cha* 𐨖 no doubt looks like the Kṣatrapa sign for four. But the Indian words for four, all begin with the unaspirated *ca*. Again, the Aśoka signs for six (see below plate III) have on

[51] quest probably happened shortly before 500 B. C., it is impossible that the Kharoṣṭhī can have been developed before 450 B. C., and it is not to be thought of that it could have penetrated into Eastern India, where the Buddhist Canon was composed, during the fifth century, much less could it have been there in so general use, as the alphabet mentioned by the ancient Buddhists certainly was. Under the circumstances just discussed, the assumption that the alphabet, referred to in the Jātakas, the Mahāvagga and so forth is the Brāhmī—which, I repeat, the palaeographic facts contained in Aśoka's Edicts, the Indian letters on the Persian Sigloi, the legend of the Eraṇ coin, the Bhaṭṭiprolu inscriptions strongly suggest—undeniably gains a very high degree of probability.

IV.

As the literary evidence points to the common use of writing in India during the fifth and perhaps in the sixth century B. C., and as the palaeographic evidence proves the Brāhmī lipi to be the oldest Indian alphabet and to be probably identical with the script referred to in the Buddhist Canon, it is a matter of course that its source must be found in the more ancient Semitic characters. A short time ago such a result would have precluded the possibility of all attemps to make Southern Arabia the country from which the parents of the Brāhma letters came. But at present, pretensions to a high antiquity are put

---

resemblance to the Kharoṣṭhī *sa* . Further the Kṣatrapa sign for seven or Gupta cannot be the Kharoṣṭhī palatal *śa* , because the word for seven begins in all Indian dialects with a dental *sa*. Again, the Kṣatrapa and Andhra cannot represent the Kharoṣṭhī *Aś*, because no such ligature is ever formed in any Indian writing. Besides, if it had been formed, it would be wrong. The second part ought to be the lingual *ṣa* , because the word is *aṣṭan* not *aśṭan*. Finally, the nought of the ninth and later centuries O cannot be derived from a sign for 10 expressed by a circle, because no such figure exists, nor from the entirely dissimilar Kharoṣṭhī *da* . The Hindus call the nought explicitly *śūnyabindu* "the dot marking a blank", and about A. D. 500 they marked it by a simple dot, which latter is commonly used in inscriptions and MSS in order to mark a blank (see the Grundriss, I, 11, pp. 78 and 86), and which was later converted into a small circle.

forward on behalf of various epigraphic documents from the latter country. The theories, it is true, are still conflicting. Some ascribe certain Sabaean inscriptions to the tenth century B. C. or an earlier period, while others declare those of the Minaeans to belong to very ancient times and deny the antiquity of the Sabaean documents. More light on these questions is required, but even as matters stand at present, it seems to me hazardous to make use of the old argument, that the derivation of the Brāhma letters from a South-Arabian source is *a priori* impossible, because the inscriptions, found there, are of too modern dates.

[52] Nevertheless the theory of a South-Semitic origin of the Brāhma alphabet appears to me untenable. What has been brought forward in its favour by the two chief advocates, is to a great extent far from convincing. The ocular evidence, it seems to me, speaks against many of their identifications.[1] Further, in some cases late or at least secondary forms of Indian letters have been used for comparison.[2] Again in other cases the most extraordinary and absolutely unnecessary changes in the phonetic value of the signs are assumed to be quite natural and hardly worthy of an explanatory remark. When one is told that the Hindus utilised the Semitic *Qoph* to express the sound *cha* (Deecke) or *cha* and *ka* (Taylor), that they employed the Semitic *Shin* for *ja, śa, ṣa* and *sa* (Deecke) or at least for *ja* and *ṣa* (Taylor), that the Semitic *Wāw* furnished both the signs for *ya* and *va,* or that *Lamed* became *ra* and *Resh* was turned into *la,* one can only say that such assertions are hard to believe. As the Hindus are always very particular, even pedantic, in matters connected with phonetics, and as the framers of the Brāhmī lipi evidently have been careful with respect to the formation of many derivative signs, duly deriving *ḍha* from *ḍa, pha* from *pa, bha* from *ba* and so forth, it seems incredible that they should have had no regard for phonetic affinities in utilising the signs, which they borrowed. And the assumed vagaries appear absolutely inexplicable if

[1] That is also Sir A. Cunningham's statement, Coins of Ancient India, pp. 39—40.

[2] To the former class belong Dr. Deecke's initial *A* and Dr. Taylor's broad-backed *śa,* to the latter Dr. Taylor's initial *A*, *kha* and *ra.*

one considers that the Semitic alphabet has the *Tsade,* the phonetic value of which comes close to *ca* and *cha,* and that it possesses separate signs for *Wāw* and *Yod,* which might be used to express *va* and *ya.*

As long as the theories regarding the derivation of the Brāhma alphabet contain equations like those just mentioned, and as long as these theories do not take into account all the oldest forms of the Indian letters, the problem, it seems to me, has not been solved and the task has to be redone. Really trustworthy results can only be attained under the following conditions:—

[53] (1) The comparison must be based on the oldest forms of the Indian alphabet and actually occurring Semitic signs of one and the same period.

(2) The comparison may include only such irregular equations, as can be supported by analogies from other cases, where nations have borrowed foreign alphabets.

(3) The comparison must show that there are fixed principles of derivation.

In resuming the inquiry on these principles I soon found that the Southern Semitic characters would not serve my purpose. Though the Himyaritic or Sabaean alphabet on account of its stiff, monumental appearance bears a general resemblance to the *Brāhmī lipi,* and though two or three of its letters come close to the corresponding Indian signs, it includes so many dissimilar characters, which evidently are more strongly modified than the Brāhma Mātṛkās, that the real resemblances can only be considered as accidental or as due to an analogous development. But on trying the oldest characters, which are almost identical throughout all the countries, occupied by the Northern Semites, it became possible to identify in the Brāhma alphabet all the twenty two Semitic letters, and to explain the formation of the numerous derivative signs, which the Indians were compelled to add. As stated already, the identifications agree for the greater part with Professor Weber's, whose important essay in the Zeitschrift der Deutschen Morgenländischen Gesellschaft of 1855 very nearly solved the problem of the origin of the Brāhma alphabet. If Professor Weber had had at his disposal the materials which are accessible at present, his acumen would no doubt have removed every difficulty.

The identifications are shown in the accompanying Table, kindly drawn for me by Mr. S. Pepper and etched by Messrs Angerer and Göschl of Vienna. The signs of the first two columns have been taken from M. Ph. Berger's Histoire de l'Écriture dans l'Antiquité, pp. 185 and 202 and those of Col. III with the exception of the Tāw from Sinjirli (22. III. b) from Professor Euting's Tabula Scripturae Aramaicae (1890). Among the forms of column IV without asterisks, those opposite the twelfth and the seventeenth Semitic characters [54] have been taken from a plaster cast of Sir A. Cunningham's Eraṇ coin (see also Coins of Ancient India, plate XI, 18) and that opposite the sixteenth character from the word *eṣā* in the Kālsī version, Ed. XIII, 1, l. 37.

Among the signs in column V and VI a few are from Sānchi, viz. the lingual *ḷa,* the fifth of Col. VI opposite the fourth Semitic character, and the first of Col. V opposite the sixteenth Semitic character. Further, in Col. VI the fourth sign opposite the sixth Semitic character, *Ū,* comes from Bharahut, the first opposite No 15 from the Eraṇ coin the third opposite the fifteenth Semitic character in Col. VI has been taken from the Ghasundi slab, and two signs of the two rows in the same Col. opposite the sixteenth character, viz. the second in the first row, *AI,* and the last in the second row, *Ī,* belong to the Hathigumphā and Nānāghāt inscriptions. All the remaining letters have been drawn according to Dr. Burgess' facsimiles of the Rock and Pillar Edicts,[1] and of the Bhaṭṭiprolu inscriptions.

A. The Borrowed Signs.

Before proceeding to the details, it will be desirable to state the principles, on which the twenty-two signs of the Semitic alphabet seem to have been turned into Brāhma letters. Even a superficial examination of the Brāhma alphabet shows the following chief characteristics:—

(1) The letters are set up as straight as possible, and they are with few exceptions made equal in height.

---

[1] The facsimiles of the Girnār and Kālsī versions, on which I have chiefly drawn, have been published, Epigr. Ind. vol. II, p. 447 ff. The Pillar Edicts have appeared *op. cit.,* p. 245 ff. and the Bhaṭṭiprolu inscriptions *op. cit.* p. 323 ff.

(2) The majority consists of vertical lines with appendages attached mostly at the foot, occasionally at the foot and at the top, or rarely in the middle; but there is no case where an appendage has been added to the top alone.

[55] (3) At the top of the characters appear mostly the ends of vertical lines, less frequently straight horizontal lines, still more rarely curves or the points of angles opening downwards, and quite exceptionally in *ma* (No 13, Col. V) two lines rising upwards. In no case does the top show several angles, placed side by side, with a vertical or slanting line hanging down from it, or a triangle or circle with a pendant line.

The principles or tendencies, which produced these characteristics, seem to be a certain pedantic formalism, a desire to have signs well suited for the formation of regular lines, and a strong aversion against all top-heavy characters.[1] The natural result was that a number of the Semitic signs had to

---

[1] The appearance of a pedantic formalism in the alphabet is no more than what might be expected. For it is a characteristic of most Indian creations in literature, science and art. The aversion, shown by the Hindus against letters with heavy tops, has also a good and sufficient reason, and, I think, it is chiefly due to their making the letters hang down from a top-line instead of placing them on a base-line (see, Bērūnī, India I, 172). The modern Karkun or clerk of Western, and, as Dr. Grierson informs me, also of Eastern India, as a rule, actually draws this line across the whole breadth of the paper, and the modern Lekhak or copyist places a small board with thin threads fastened at equal distances below his sheet of paper, or squeezes the paper between the strings and the board. The general appearance of the most ancient MSS., like the Bower birch bark volume and the Horiuzi palmleaves, makes it highly probable that their writers used the same or a similar contrivance. Even the look of the Aśoka inscriptions, especially of the Pillar Edicts and of the Girnār and Jaugada Rock Edicts, indicates that their engravers, or the writers of the original copies, were accustomed to the use of top lines. Though they are rarely quite exact, it is clearly visible that they at least tried to equalise the height of the tops. If the custom, as is not improbable, dates from still earlier times, the aversion against heavy tops is easily explained. For signs beginning with vertical lines or with short horizontal strokes are most suitable for such writing, and the later modifications of the Brāhma letters are to a great extent the results of a variety of attempts to obtain such forms. Another reason may have been the introduction of the vowel-signs, which mostly are added to the tops of the consonants.

be turned topsy-turvy or to be laid on their sides, while the triangles or double angles, occurring at the tops of others had to be got rid of by some contrivance or other. A further change in the position of the signs had to be made, when the Hindus began to write from the left to the right. They had, of course, to be turned from the right to the left, as in Greek. [56] Instances, where the old position has been preserved, are however met with both in borrowed and derivative signs.

With respect to the single borrowed letters I have to add the following remarks.

No 1. That the Hindus, like the Greeks used the Semitic *Aleph* in order to express the vowel *a* has been suspected by Professor Weber. His successors have asserted the identity of the first letters of the two alphabets as a fact, though the Indian forms of the initial *A* with two curves, which have been mostly used for comparison,[1] do not agree very well. The doubtlessly oldest form with the angle to the left of the vertical (Col. V) which, as stated above, is peculiar to the Southern versions of the Edicts, agrees almost exactly with the oldest Semitic signs. Only the vertical has been placed at the point of the angle in order to make the appearance of the letter more regular, and the whole sign has, of course, been turned from the right to the left. On a Patna seal it occurs, however, once in its original position, see the Grundriss, Taf. II. 1. I, and p. 8.

No 2. I can only agree to the identification of the Brāhma *ba* with the Semitic *Beth*, which has been asserted on the strength of the Sabaean and Ethiopian forms[2] by Professor Weber and his successors, with the exception of M. Halévy, who derives it from the dissimilar Greek *Beta*. But I think that it is a development, derived by the Hindus immediately from the

---

[1] M. Halévy, however, correctly compares the angular form. His attempt to derive it from the Greek Alpha is not intelligible to me. The two signs possess a minimum of resemblance to each other.

[2] The Sabaean form is no doubt very similar to the Brāhma sign but, I think, due to a different modification of the ancient North Semitic letter. It would seem that the triangle at the head of the letter has been turned into a square and the stroke on the right has been made straight. Hence arose first the and by a simplification .

old Phoenician and Mesa signs. As the Hindus did not tolerate heavy tops, they opened the triangle and made the central stroke hang down from the end of the angle in the manner shown in the hypothetical form in Col. III.[1] The next result was a rhomboid form (Col. V, a), a few examples of which are found occasionally in various versions of the Edicts, where we have *e. g.* 𑀩𑁄 *bo* in *apalibodhāye,* Kālsī Edict V, l. 15. The liking of the
[57] Hindus for straight top-lines produced further the square and the oblong *ba,* which latter is the commonest form in Kālsī and the regular one in the Bhaṭṭiprolu inscriptions. It may be noted, that this letter is frequently, though not regularly, made smaller than those with verticals. Regarding the want of the lower line in the derivative *bha* (Col. VI) see below.

No 3. The identity of the Indian *ga* with the Semitic signs is so evident that it has been always recognised. I will only add that there are numerous instances in the Edicts where one of the sides of the angle is shorter than the other. The formal looking very pointed angles with perfectly straight equal sides are characteristic of the Western and Southern versions.

No 4. The identity of the Brāhma *dha* with the Semitic *Daleth* has also been generally admitted, Dr. Taylor, who derives it from *tha* (No 9, Col. V) alone dissenting. To me it seems that the first form, given in Col. V, with the vertical on the right, is the immediate offspring of the oldest Semitic forms, the letter having been made higher and the right hand stroke straightened in accordance with the general principles of formation, stated, above. The round back is probably due to a cursive development. In the Edicts this form is rare, and the second, given in Col. V, which is younger and due to the change in the position required by the change in the direction of the writing, is found in the great majority of cases. The older one (Col. V, a) is used exclusively in the Bhaṭṭiprolu inscriptions and usually in the Western cave inscriptions of the Nānāghāt, Nasik, Karle, Junnar and so forth, which range from about 150 B. C. to 200 A. D. It is also the parent of all the later

[1] An apparently analogous modification of the old Semitic Beth which one might be inclined to see in the b² 𐰋 of the Orkhon inscriptions (V. Thomsen, Inscr. de l'Orkhon déchiffrées, p. 24) is disposed of by Prof. Donner's remarks on the sign in his essay, sur l'origine de l'Alphabet Turc, p. 57 f.

northern forms of the letter, including the present Devanāgarī *dha.* In the caves mentioned we find also in the Andhra and other inscriptions of the first and second centuries A. D. numerous triangular forms[1] like ◁ or △. They may be possibly ancient survivals, especially as the Edicts too occasionally offer forms with half angular backs like D.

The difficulty with respect to the phonetic value of the Brāhma sign, which does not exactly correspond to that of [58] the *Daleth,* may perhaps be explained by the suggestion that the letter was used for a long time both for the unaspirated and the aspirated dental, and that the *da* was separated at a time, when the real value of the borrowed sign had been forgotten.

No 5. Professor Weber denies the connexion of the Brāhma *ha* with the Semitic *He,* while Drs. Deecke and Taylor derive it from the Sabaean form Ч.[2] As long as only the round form, given as the third sign in Col. V, and similar ones were known to exist in the Edicts, the case was a difficult one. Dr. Burgess' new impressions and facsimiles show, however, that the angular *ha,* Col. V, b, which is constant in the cave inscriptions of the next centuries, occurs here and there in Aśoka's inscriptions.[3] The new Siddāpur version shows throughout the little horizontal bar (on the right) attached very close to the foot of the letter and offers in the word *mahātpane* No. I, l. 4) the sign, placed first in Col. V. This is almost exactly a turned *He* of the Assyrian weights (Col. III, b) which according to M. de Vogüé[4] appears from about 700 B. C. Professor Euting kindly points out to me that the very similar *He* of Col. III, 1 is found on a *Mina* (C. I. S., P. II, No 6^b), which according to the accompanying cuneiform inscription dates from the reign of Salmanassar, and therefore, as also M. de Vogüé has stated in his remarks on the inscription, is older

---

[1] See Burgess, Arch. Surv. Reports West-Ind., Vol. IV, Plates XLIV, 17; XLVIII, 16, 17; and the Grundriss, I, 11, Tafel III. 24. VII, XI.

[2] This sign is due to a very much stronger modification of the ancient North-Semitic *He* than the Brāhma letter.

[3] See also above p. 41, and the Grundriss, Tafel II. 40. VI.

[4] Corpus Inscr. Semit., P. II, Vol. I, p. III. Mr. Berger enters this sign (Table, op. cit., p. 300) in the column for the Persian period.

than the year 725 B. C. As this sign belongs to the eighth century B. C., when the very archaic forms of the *Aleph, Daleth, Cheth, Theth, Waw* and *Qoph,* represented by the corresponding Brāhma letters, still existed,[1] it may be considered the prototype of the Indian *ha.* The aversion of the Hindus against heavy tops, of course, caused the sign to be turned round, and their liking for regularity caused the bar to be attached to the stroke which then became the base-line, and the whole letter to be set up straight. All things considered, this explanation seems [59] more probable than attempts to connect *ha* with the later more exactly agreeing sign in Col. III, b, or with the still older form with three parallel bars.

No 6. The Indian *va,* regarding which Professor Weber felt uncertain, evidently corresponds with the Mesa form of *Wāw.* Owing to the aversion against heavy tops the Semitic letter has been turned topsy-turvy. At the same time the semicircle has been closed. Among the two forms, given in Col. V, the second is the regular one in the Edicts, the first, as well as an angular variety not given,[2] occurs only rarely.

No 7. Professor Weber has already pronounced himself for the identity of the Brāhma *ja* with the *Zain.* On phonetic grounds Professor Weber's conjecture is extremely probable. For, ever since the Indians began to borrow Persian and Arabic words, they have rendered the *Zain* of the latter by their *ja,* and the dictionaries of the Indian vernaculars contain hundreds of instances of this kind. Even in earlier times, about A. D. 500, they express, *e. g.* in *jīva* for Ζεύς *(Ziv-s)* the Greek *Zeta,* which then had the value of Zain, by *ja.* Both facts prove that the two sounds had a close affinity for their ear. The discovery of the Bhaṭṭiprolu *j,*[3] Col. V, a, considerably facilitates the identification of the two signs, as it closely agrees with the archaic Phoenician sign, differing only slightly in the position of the bars at the top and the foot. The signs of the

[1] See M. de Vogüé, op. cit., p. II.

[2] Compare also above p. 41, where a fourth cursive form has been figured.

[3] Dr. Burgess' facsimiles in the Epigraphia Indica show occasionally an incipient central bar in *ju* and *jū,* where it ought not to occur. The impressions prove clearly that in all these cases there is not a real third line, but that the stone has a flaw.

Edicts, given in Col. V, b—d, are all cursive, and represent attempts to make the letter with a single stroke or at least with two. The third form with a dot at the junction of the two curves, is of course a development from the second with the loop. And the substitution of a dot for a loop indicates that the persons who invented it wrote with pen and ink. A man working with a stylus would not think of such a substitution, nay could hardly effect it.[1]

No 8. The discovery of the angular *gha* (Col. V, a) which occurs a few times in the Kālsī version[2] and is constant in the cave inscriptions, makes its identification with the three-barred [60] *Cheth* of the archaic Phoenician, of the Sinjirli and other ancient inscriptions, very probable. The Semitic sign, which often slants towards the left, has been laid on its side (see the hypothetical form in Col. IV) and the long upper bar, covering the letter, has been raised upwards and converted into the long vertical on the left.[3] The usual form of the Aśoka Edicts with the curve is of course cursive. In the Bhaṭṭiprolu alphabet this letter has been discarded and a derivative from *ga* (No 3, Col. VI) takes its place. The Sabaean *Cheth* Ψ, from which Dr. Taylor derives the Indian *gha*, is no doubt an analogous development from the old North-Semitic sign.

No 9. The identity of the Brāhma *tha* with the Semitic *Theth* has always been recognised and is evident enough. I may mention as a curiosity that a small cross appears inside the circle instead of a dot in the Pallava landgrant, Epigraphia Indica, Vol. I, p. 1 ff. In this document all dots are replaced

---

[1] Regarding the use of ink in India, see above p. 22. The ancient Indian term for ink is *maṣi*, often spelt *masi*, and now pronounced *makhi*, which is derived from the obsolete verb *maṣ, hiṃsāyām*, compare *maṣa* and *maṣmaṣā*. Etymologically and originally it means 'powder' (of charcoal and the like), used for the preparation of ink, see the larger Petersburg Dictionary under *masi*, and the Grundriss, I, 11, p. 91.

[2] The sign given in the Table has been taken from *upaghāte*, Ed. XIII, 1, l. 37.

[3] It may be mentioned as a curiosity, that from the twelfth century A. D. the Nāgarī *gha* is again placed upright and has become almost identical with its Semitic prototype, see the Grundriss, Taf. V. 13. XX—XXII. This is, however, not due to a survival, but merely to the desire of equalising the breadth of the Nāgarī letters.

by minute crosses. On the other hand, a *Theth* with a dot occurs on an Assyrian weight, see Col. III.

No 10. The derivation of the Brāhma *ya* from the ancient Semitic *Yod* has been asserted by Professor Weber, who however could only compare the later round Phoenician form, which opens downwards.[1] The oldest Indian form is probably the notched one (Col. V, a),[2] which appears exclusively in the Delhi Pillar Edicts and occasionally in most other versions and is the parent of all the later developments. It is probably derived from the oldest Semitic *Yod,* formed of a downstroke with two bars, attached to the left, and one to the right. Its formation seems to have been effected by placing the top-heavy sign on its side, in the manner shown in the hypothetical form of [61] Col. III, by lengthening the stroke which now stood in the middle of the line and equalising the direction of that on the right.

No 11. The derivation of the Brāhma *ka* was a difficult problem, as long as the cross with four perfectly equal bars (Col. V, b) was considered to be its most ancient form, and consequently the earlier attempts to account for its existence are not very satisfactory. Professor Weber, following Kopp, and Dr. Taylor have tried to derive it from the Semitic *Qoph* very much against the ocular evidence, and M. Halévy has identified it with the Aramaic *Kaph,* which likewise, as far as I can see, does not resemble the Indian letter. But now, when the more accurate reproductions of the Edicts have proved the frequent early occurrence of the dagger-shaped form (Col. V, a) which is constant in Bhaṭṭiprolu and in *all* the various inscriptions, incised between 200 B. C. and 550 A. D., the case of the sign is by no means desperate nor even difficult. If, as now may be done with perfect propriety, the dagger-shaped *ka* is taken as the older form and the cross with equal bars as a regularised or formalised derivative, it is easily recognisable that the dagger-form probably has been derived from a *Kaph,* like that of Mesa's inscription (Col. II), in which the down-

[1] Is has also been admitted by M. Halévy, who compares a late form of the Semitic letter.

[2] That with the single curved stroke at the foot of the vertical is apparently cursive.

stroke slants sharply to the left and the angle on the left is attached very close to the top, compare also the signs of the Siloah inscription, in Prof. Euting's Tabula Script. Aram. Col. 3. In setting the sign up straight, the Hindus took the upper stroke of the angle for the top of the down-stroke, and a cross-like figure was the natural result, which, on being made more regular, yielded the dagger-shape.

No 12. For the identity of the Brāhma *la* (Col. V, a) with the Semitic *Lamed* (Cols. I and II), which has been recognised by Professor Weber and accepted by Dr. Deecke and M. Halévy, the *la* of the Eraṇ coin (Col. IV), the Bhaṭṭiprolu *la* (Col. V, b) and the Bhaṭṭiprolu *ḷ* (Col. VI) furnish new illustrations. The most ancient survival is found in the last mentioned character, which, if the little bar denoting the lingualisation is removed, almost exactly represents the Semitic sign. Next comes the letter of the Eraṇ coin, which has pre-[62] served the original direction of the *Lamed*, but shows on the right the little bar, no doubt intended to mark the end of the line. This bar is wanting in the Bhaṭṭiprolu *ḷ*, which however has been turned from the right to the left and has developed a curious long tail, hanging down from the top of the main line. Originally this appendage no doubt was a flourish, marking the end of the vertical.

No 13. The identification of the Brāhma *ma* with the Semitic *Mem* is also due to Professor Weber. He, as well as M. Halévy, derive it from the Aramaic sign of the seventh century[1] B. C., 𐡌. Though this derivation is no doubt tempting it seems to me that it is equally possible to connect the Brāhma *ma* with a sign like that of the Mesa inscription, which likewise shows a curve at the end of the down-stroke. A little stronger development of this curve would necessarily lead to a sign, like the hypothetical one, entered in Col. IV, which is almost the same as the first Pehlevī *Mem* of Col. 58 in Professor Euting's Tabula Script. Aram. And in support of this view I may appeal to the development of the looped *ka*, Northern 𑀓 and Southern 𑀓 from the dagger-shaped *ka* with a curve at he foot 𑀓, as well as of the round ad Southern *ra* 𑀭 from 𑀭, which

[1] See M. de Vogüé, loc. cit.

show analogous changes on purely Indian ground. The superposition of the angle, which originally remained at the side, over the round or elliptical figure[1] is of course due to the striving after regularity, which the Hindus show throughout. The Brāhma *ma* with the angle at the top (Col. V, a) which is (see also above p. 39) particularly common in the Girnār version and not found in the Northern versions, thus appears to be the older form, and that with a curve (Col. V, b) the cursive one. In the Bhaṭṭiprolu alphabet the ancient Brāhma *ma* with the angle appears turned topsy-turvy (see p. 46). The Sabaean, *Beta*-like *Mem,*  from which Dr. Deecke and Dr. Taylor derive the Brāhma *ma,* shows little resemblance and is probably the product of a different process.

[63] No 14. Professor Weber,[2] who is followed by Dr. Deecke, considers the Semitic *Nun* to be represented by the Brāhma *ṇa,* Col. VI, b, and it is Dr. Taylor alone who connects the dental *na,* Col. V, directly with the Sabaean form of *Nun.* I do not think it probable that a Hindu would make such a mistake as to take the phonetic value of *Nun* to be equivalent to his lingual nasal, which sounds very differently, and I fail to see, except on the impossible theory of Greek mediation, how the double horizontal line of *ṇa* can be explained by means of a real Semitic form. It seems to me that the Hindus, owing to their aversion to heavy tops, first turned the *Nun* topsy-turvy and used for some time a figure like that drawn in Col. IV.[3] As a proof for this assertion I would cite the palatal

---

[1] The third Pehlevī *Mem* of Col. 59 of the same Table, which exactly resembles the Brāhma *ma,* may be pointed out as an interesting analogous development.

[2] I must add that Professor Weber admits the possibility of deriving the dental *na* from *Nun,* but thinks that the *ṇa* comes nearer. M. Halévy connects *ṇa* immediately with the Greek νυ, which, as he believes, was laid on its side.

[3] A *Nun* with a small open square at the top, instead of an angle, occurs in the Siloah inscription and again much later, see Prof. Euting's Tabula Scr. Aram. Cols. 3a-b, 8b, and 13a. As the change from an angle to an open square is in keeping with the stiff formalism of the Indian alphabet, it is not necessary to assume that the Semitic prototype showed the latter. The Indian form is probably nothing but an analogous development.

ña (Col. VI, a), which consists of the hypothetical form, turned from right to left, and of a small bar at the top, indicating that it belongs to a different class or Varga.

Later only, I think, the Hindus substituted as a cursive development for the hook at the side, the single bar which protrudes on either side of the foot of the vertical.

No 15. Professor Weber doubtingly proposes to connect the Brāhma *sa* (Col. VI, d) with the Semitic *Samech,* and his idea has been taken up by Dr. Taylor who derives it from the very dissimilar Sabaean form ᛘ. The new Bhaṭṭiprolu *ṣ*, Col. V (the origin of which has been wrongly explained in my introductory remarks to the edition of the inscriptions) and the *sa* of the Eraṇ coin (Col. VI, a) as well as the *ṣa* of the Ghasundi slab (see below), I think, permit me to say that Professor Weber's conjecture is well founded. I take the Bhaṭṭiprolu *ṣ* to be derived from a *Samech* like that in Col. I, b, the two [64] upper bars of which were replaced by a curve (as in the hypothetical sign in Col. IV) and which was then turned topsy-turvy in accordance with the Indian principle, appealed to so often. This sign probably served in the beginning to express both *sa* and *ṣa*. Later two separate signs were developed out of this original representative for *Samech,* (1) the sign for *sa* with the original cross bar placed at the outside of the curve, which appears in its original position on the Eraṇ coin (Col. VI, a) and turned from the right to the left (Col. VI, b) in the Southern versions of the Edicts (Girnār and Siddāpur) and in Bhaṭṭiprolu; (2) the sign for *ṣa* (Col. VI, c), with the original cross-bar shortened and placed inside the curve, which hitherto is traceable only on the Ghasundi slab,[1] but must have been used extensively, as it is evidently the parent of the square *ṣa* of the later Sanskrit inscriptions.[2] It occurs neither in the Bhaṭṭiprolu alphabet, which retained the old sign, in order to denote *ṣ*, nor in the ordinary Brāhmī lipi

[1] See Journ. As. Soc. Beng., Vol. LVI, Plate at p. 79, where it occurs in the name *Saṁkarṣaṇa*.

[2] The square form occurs first in the Mora Well inscription from the times of Rājuvula's son (Śoḍāsa), Arch. Surv. Rep., Vol. XX, Plate V, 4, which possibly belongs to the first century A. D.

of the Edicts. The northern variety of the latter developed a new *sa* (Col. VI, d) with a curve instead of the straight limb at the side, and out of this the sign with two curves, one below the other (Col. VI, e), which occurs in the Kālsī version, in Daśaratha's Nāgārjunī cave inscriptions and so forth, and which probably is also intended for *ṣa*.

It would, of course, be possible to connect the Bhaṭṭiprolu *ṣ* with the cursive Aramaic *Samech* (Col. III) of the sixth century B. C. But then the cross bar of the Bhaṭṭiprolu sign would remain unexplained. Moreover, there would be the insuperable difficulty that the Aramaic *Beth, Daleth, Waw, Cheth, Ain, Qoph* and *Resh* of the sixth century are so strongly modified that they cannot be considered the prototypes of the corresponding Brāhma *ba, dha, va, gha, E, kha* and *ra*. It seems, therefore, advisable to assume, as must be done also in the case of *śa*, that the Hindus independently changed the form of the ancient sign, but in a manner analogous to that adopted by the Aramaeans.

[65] The derivation of the signs for *sa* and *ṣa* from the same original letter points to the influence of the Sanskrit grammarians or phoneticists, who are well aware of the intimate connection of the two sounds and duly teach that Sanskrit *sa* becomes *ṣa* through the influence of a preceding *i, u, ṛ, e, ai, o, au, k, r* or *l*.

No 16. Professor Weber's ingenious identification of the ancient *Ain* (Col. I and II) with the Brāhma *E*,—which is supported by the analogous proceeding of the Greeks, who also used it to express the gutturo-labial vowel, and of the modern Jews,[1] who express the *e* of foreign words by *Ain*, —receives a strong confirmation through the round and half-round signs for *E* in Col. IV and Col. V, a—b. The first occurs once in the word *eṣā*, Kālsī, Edict XIII, 1, l. 37. The same version offers also several times the very similar form[2] of Col. V, b. The first sign in Col. V,

[1] See Grierson, Ind. Ant., vol. XXIV, p. 248, Note 5. The cause of this substitution is probably the resemblance of the Hebrew ע to a cursive *e*, torned towards the left.

[2] It seems probable, that this or a similar half round form is the parent of the southern *E*, which in the Pallava and Vengi inscriptions looks like *ca*,  and later becomes , closely resembling the ancient *la*.

which looks like a *dha* is found in the word *etina* of the Hathigumphā inscription of Khāravela, l. 8, and in the Sānchi inscription No 173 (Epigraphia Indica Vol. II, p. 375) where, not thinking of the Hathigumphā letter, I unfortunately have read *Dharakinā* for *Erakinā*. Professor Weber's conjecture has been accepted by Dr. Taylor alone, Dr. Deecke and M. Halévy, trying to connect the triangular *E* with *Aleph*. There was however a very good reason for giving up the round *E*. For it could not have been distinguished from the lingual *ṭha*, which the Hindus developed out of the corresponding dental. In my opinion the triangular *E* is a development, formed by the Hindus independently, and the angular forms for *Ain* in the later Semitic alphabets, Euting op. cit., Col. 8 b, 14 ff., are merely analogous, showing how easily a circular letter may be converted into a triangle or rhombus. It is just possible that phonetic considerations may have induced the Indians to select *Ain* for expressing their *e*. For according to a description of the Indian *e*-sound, which seems to go back to Śākaṭāyana and has been generally accepted by the later native grammarians,[1] it is half guttural and half palatal (*kaṇṭhya-tālavya*). As the *Ain* no doubt was a guttural, it may have appeared more suitable for *E* than for *I* or *U*.

No 17. The fact that the Brāhma *pa* is the old Semitic *Phe* turned topsy-turvy, has been acknowledged by everybody. The new form of the Eraṇ coin, Col. IV, shows it in its original position.

No 18. Regarding the Brāhma equivalent of the Semitic *Tsade* I differ from all my predecessors. I believe that it was [66] used, as one would expect from its phonetic value, for the formation of the letter *ca*, the sound of which is and always has been, not the English *tsha*, but *t́sa* almost like *tya*. The Semitic sign, of course, had to be turned topsy-turvy on account of its heavy top, and the small bar running to the right was turned towards the vertical. This process gave first a tailed  and later with the direction to the left, 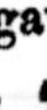. The angular shape of the letter has been well preserved in the *ca* of the Edicts, Col. V, a, which is not uncommon, and the tail appears

[1] See Weber, Indische Studien, vol. IV, p. 119 f.

in the Bhaṭṭiprolu form, Col. V, c.[1] The round *ca* (Col. V, b) is purely cursive, and not the parent of the later Indian letters, which mostly go back to angular or pointed forms.

No 19. With respect to the Semitic *Qoph* I must likewise differ from all my predecessors, who have compared it to the Brāhma *cha*, which is clearly an Indian derivative from *ca* and has a very different phonetic value. In my opinion the Semitic *Qoph* has its counterpart in the Brāhma *kha*, the oldest form of which (Col. V, a) consists of a circle with a superimposed vertical line ending in a curve. This is the oldest Semitic sign (Cols. I and II),[2] turned topsy-turvy on account of its heavy top. The curve at the end of the vertical has no doubt been added in order to distinguish the letter from *va*. The *kha* with the circle at the base occurs sometimes in Jaugada and is used frequently in the Kālsī version[3] of the Edicts, where not rarely the circle is replaced by a somewhat irregular loop, sometimes attached to the right of the vertical line (see the *kha* figured above p. 41). It is the parent of most of the later Indian signs for *kha*, including the modern Devanāgarī form, which all show a loop or a triangle at the base of the vertical. In several versions of the Pillar [67] Edicts and elsewhere a well developed dot takes the place of the circle. This change is analogous to that pointed out above in connexion with the second and third forms of the Brāhma *ja*, and likewise indicates the use of pen and ink for the time when it was made. There is also a third form of the *kha* which consists merely of a vertical with a hook at the top. It is chiefly used in the Southern versions of the Edicts, particularly in Girnār, as well as in Bhaṭṭiprolu and later in the cave inscriptions, and is evidently a cursive development.

---

[1] The later Semitic alphabets furnish various analogous developments, see Prof. Euting's Tabula, Col. 9 (third sign), Col. 15 (first sign), Col. 42 (second sign), differing from the Brāhma letter only by the position of the angular or round appendage, which of course remains at the top of the character and to the right of the vertical stroke.

[2] Still more closely agreeing Phoenician and Mesa forms, in which the vertical is not drawn across the round head, are given in Prof. Euting's Tabula, Col. 1*d*, Col. 2*a*.

[3] The form given in the plate has been taken from the word *likhite*, Kālsī, Edict IV, l. 12 (end).

In favour of this identification speaks also the fact that the modern Indians in loan words not rarely express the Arabic *Qoph* by their *kha*. Thus the Marāṭhī has खिस्त, खिस्ता, खुमास, खुरनाण, खूम and so forth for Arabic words with *Qoph*. This substitution shows that the Indian ear detects an affinity between the deep guttural *Qoph* and the harsh sounding *kha*.

No 20. I can only agree with Professor Weber's identification of *Resh* with the Brāhma *ra* or *repha*. But the original *ra* has not the form, consisting of a straight stroke, which is given in his table and in that of Dr. Taylor. The straight *ra*, evidently a late cursive development, is very rare in the Edicts. I know only of one instance in the Rūpnāth Edict in which a nearly straight stroke occurs. In the Girnār version, where *ra* is very common, it has at the top invariably one or two little angles, open to the right, or instead of the angle an irregular bulge towards the left, see Col. V, a—b. I take the form with the single angle to be the oldest and consider it to be derived from a Semitic form like that of the Mesa inscription, the triangle of which the Hindus opened, in order to avoid the heavy top, by attaching the vertical to the lower side of the base *i. e.* by putting  for . The signs with two or more angles, Col. V, d—e, are no doubt artificial, ornamental developments. In the new Siddāpur Edicts this development has been carried to an extreme, and the whole letter has been converted into a wavy line, consisting of four or five little angles.

No 21. Professor Weber's identification of *Shin* with the palatal sibilant *śa,* which has been accepted by Dr. Deecke, seems also to me self-evident. It is only necessary to substitute for the late Indian form (given in Professor Weber's Col. II) the formerly not accessible, real old Brāhma signs, Col. V, a—c, which are found in the Kālsī, Rūpnāth and Siddāpur versions of the Edicts, on the Bhaṭṭiprolu prism, on the Ghasundi slab and in the Pabhosa cave inscriptions.[1] I con-

[1] I enumerate the occurrences so fully, because, when the sign first turned up in Kālsī, it was considered to have been borrowed from the Kharoṣṭhī, which has the remotely similar lingual *ṣa* 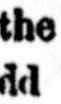. I will add that in Bhaṭṭiprolu where we have *śamaṇudeśānaṃ i. e. śramaṇoddeśyānām,* in the Ghasundi inscription where we have *Parāśariputa* and *śilā,* and in

[68] sider as their prototype the oldest Semitic form with two angles (Cols. I and II), not the very similar Aramaic *Shin* (Col. III) of the sixth century. For in accordance with the principles of the Brāhmī lipi, the Semitic letter had to be turned topsy-turvy, and the double angle at the top had to be got rid of, which latter change could be most easily effected by placing the one angle inside the other. The Hindus may be well credited with the independent invention of this modification, as the later Phoenicians and the Ethiopians have likewise introduced it independently. Moreover, the same considerations, which make it impossible to accept the Aramaic *Samech* as the immediate source of the Bhaṭṭiprolu *ṣ* (see above p. 67), speak in this case against the assumption that the Semitic alphabet, adopted by the Hindus, contained the Aramaic *Shin*. Finally the Western letter-numeral *śu* for 100, still shows the two angles quite plainly, see App. II, pl. III and the Grundriss, Taf. IX, Cols. IV—V, XI.

No 22. The oldest form of the Brāhma *ta*, which Professor Weber has recognised already as a modification of the Semitic *Taw*, seems to be that (Col. V, a) consisting of a long slightly inclined downstroke with a short straight bar slanting off to the right. Next comes the sign, given in Col. V, b, with the bar slanting off to the left, and this is due to the change in the direction of the writing. The *ta* consisting of a vertical stroke with an angle at the foot, Col. V, c, which is frequent in the southern and western versions of the Edicts and also on the Sohgaurā Plate, is probably [69] due to the formalism of the

---

Pabhosa which offers *Śonakāyana i. e. Śaunakāyana*, this sign appears only in words which have *śa* in Sanskrit, while in the Edicts it occurs mostly and very irregularly in words, where the Sanskrit has *sa* or *ṣa*. The confusion is owing to the negligent pronunciation and writing of the clerk, who made the copy. His dialect probably contained two sibilants, the dental and the palatal, and his alphabet had three, the dental, the palatal and the lingual. His negligence in pronunciation made him pronounce *sa* for *śa* and vice versa, and his negligence in writing made him use *sa* and *śa* indiscriminately. As stated above, papers written in our times by half-educated clerks and others show exactly the same confusion and for the same reasons. They pronounce *e. g.* both *sac* and *śac (satyam)* and they write indiscriminately सच, शच and षच.

Hindus, their desire to set the letter up straight and to make it perfectly regular in appearance. The forms with a round limb to the right or left of the vertical (see above p. 41) of course are cursive. The oldest among these five forms for *ta* closely resembles the *Taw* from the earliest Sinjirli inscription (Col. III, b), which belongs to the beginning of the eighth century B. C., and still more that of Col. III, a, which occurs on an Assyrian weight of the reign of Salmanassar[1] and has therefore been engraved before 725 B. C. As it thus appears that Semitic forms, consisting of a long inclined downstroke with a crossbar very slightly protruding on the left or with a simple bar on the right, have been developed in very early times, it is not improbable, that one of them occurred in the alphabet which the Hindus borrowed. But the possibility that the Indian sign is an independent development from the straight Phoenician cross (Col. I), is not altogether excluded. For the cross could not remain in the Brāhma alphabet, because it would have been undistinguishable from *ka*.

B. The Derivative Consonants and Initial Vowels.

The contrivances, by which the derivative signs, both primary and secondary, for consonants and initial vowels have been formed, are:—

(1) the transposition of one of the elements of a phonetically cognate borrowed sign,

(2) the mutilation of a borrowed letter or of another derivative sign of similar phonetic value,

(3) the addition of straight lines, curves or hooks to borrowed or derivative signs. If a hook is added the original sign suffers a slight mutilation.

Two cases of transposition have already been mentioned above under No 15, where it has been pointed out that the *sa* and the Ghasundi *ṣa* come from the Bhaṭṭiprolu *ṣ*. A second case occurs, as Professor Weber has been the first to recognise, in the dental *da* (No 4, Col. VI, a—b, f—g). The

---

[1] As Professor Euting kindly points out to me, the inscription is found Corp. Inscr. Sem., P. II, No 2c.

[70] two first forms, one of which occurs in Bhaṭṭiprolu as well as on a Patna seal[1] and the other in the majority of the Edicts, are derived from the two *dha* in Col. V, by dividing the straight line and pushing the halves back to the ends of the semicircle which remained. In the third actual form (Col. VI, f) and the hypothetical one, Col. VI, g (required on account of the next following sign) the semicircle has been converted into a small square, left open on one side, and this change is due to the liking for angular forms, mentioned above p. 37.

The cases in which a borrowed or derivative sign has been mutilated, are those of the lingual *tenuis*, *tenuis aspirata* and *media*, all of which Professor Weber has already explained correctly. The lingual *ḍa* under No 4, Col. VI, c, which occurs occasionally in Kālsī and commonly in the later inscriptions of the Nānāghāt and the other Western caves etc., is derived, by the removal of the lower end, from the Bhaṭṭiprolu *da* (Col. VI, a), which had not yet been turned from the right to the left. The angular *ḍa* (Col. VI, h) comes in like manner from an angular *da* (not yet turned to the left), of which the known inscriptions do not offer any example. The *ṭha* (No 9, Col. VI, a) is of course the dental *tha* minus the central dot, and the *ṭa* (No 9, Col. VI, b) has probably been obtained by halving the *ṭha*, as Professor Weber conjectures. To a Hindu this process probably appeared very natural. For he formed several aspirates by adding curves. Hence he may be supposed to have considered a round sign, denoting an aspirate, as equivalent to an unaspirated letter *plus* a curve of aspiration. Thus the division of the sign would be quite legitimate. In the Edicts both *ṭha* and *ṭa* are frequently made smaller than the other letters.

Two other cases of the mutilation of borrowed letters occur in the signs for initial *I* and *U*. It has been recognised already by Mr. Prinsep that the three dots of *I* (No 16, Col. VI, a—c, lower row) indicate the three corners of the triangular *E*, and this view, which has been generally accepted, is confirmed by the fact, that in the Edicts the position of the dots

[1] Cunningham, Arch. Survey Rep., vol. XV, pl. III (first figure).

of *I* generally agrees with the position of the angles of *E*. To a Hindu phoneticist or grammarian the derivation of *I* from *E* would appear a matter of course, because *E* is very commonly [71] the representative of an *I* in strong forms or its *Guṇa*. Hence he expressed the latter by a lighter form of the former, just marking the corners of the triangle.

The case of *U* (No 6, Col. VI, a) is somewhat different. It has been customary to derive the sign directly from one of the later forms of the Semitic *Waw*. Considering the facts, connected with the linguals and with initial *I*, I would propose to derive it either directly from the old Semitic *Waw*, turned topsy-turvy, or from the Brāhma *va* by a bisection of the circle at the foot of the sign and the substitution of a straight line for the irregular pendant, which remained. The several steps were, therefore,  or , , , and finally[1] . It is probable that phonetic considerations, the observation of the frequent substitution of *u* for *va* in weak verbal and nominal forms, as in *uhyate, upyate, supyate, upta, supta, uṣita,* from *vah, vap, svap* and *vas,* may have led to the adoption of this proceeding. The framers of the Brāhma alphabet were, as pointed out already, Brahmans, acquainted with phonetics and with grammatical theories.

The last case of mutilation, I believe, occurs in the Anusvāra (No 13, Col. VI, b) which is represented by a simple dot. This is no doubt a substitute for the small circle (Col. VI, a), which reappears very commonly in certain later epigraphic and literary alphabets. I consider the circle to be a mutilated minute *ma,* the upper angle of which was omitted,[2] and I believe that this conjecture is supported by the following facts. In the Edicts and all other ancient inscriptions the Anusvāra is placed rarely at the top of the letter after which it is pronounced. Usually

---

[1] The former actual existence of the third form is proved by the Jaugada *O* (No 6, Col. VI, f). In the second century A. D. and later, the *U* frequently shows a curve at the foot instead of the straight line,  and it is possible that this may be an ancient survival, not, as is usually assumed, a modern development.

[2] I must acknowledge that M. Halévy's ingenious, but erroneous, conjecture, according to which the Brāhma Anusvāra is derived from the Kharoṣṭhī *ma,* induced me to frame my theory.

and regularly it stands opposite the middle, but in a number of cases it is found also to the right of the foot. Now vowelless consonants always stand at the foot of the preceding sign in the oldest Sanskrit or Mixed inscriptions from the times of the [72] Kuṣana kings down to the fifth century A. D., when the *Virāma* makes first its appearance. Moreover all such vowelless consonants are made exceedingly small, even after the invention of the *Virāma*, and they are very commonly mutilated at the top.[1] These facts would fully explain the use of a small circle for a vowelless *ma* of the Aśoka type, which then became the general sign of nasalisation in the Brāhma alphabet, just as the Kharoṣṭhī *ma* was turned into the Kharoṣṭhī Anusvāra. My theory, of course, rests on the assumption that the Brāhma alphabet was used from the beginning, not for Prakrit, but for Sanskrit, and this is made more than probable by the occurrence of *ṅa* in the Mahābodhi Gayā alphabet of the masons, as well as by the arrangement of its letters on phonetic principles, see above p. 33, likewise by the numerous indications that the alphabet was elaborated by phoneticists or grammarians, *i. e.*, by Brahman schoolmen.

Short straight strokes marking the additional *mātrā*, are added (originally on the left[2]) to the vowel-signs for *A* and *U* in order to frame the signs for the long vowels *Ā* (No 1, Col. VI) and *Ū* (No 6, Col. VI, d). In long *Ī* an additional dot appears instead of the stroke which would not have agreed with the character of the sign.[3]

Added to vowel-signs (originally on the right), short strokes indicate a change of the quality of the sound. This is the way

---

[1] See *e. g.* Epigr. Ind. II, p. 208, Mathurā Inscr., New Ser., No 27, Dr. Fleet's Gupta Inscr., Nos 3, 6, 11, etc., Dr. Hoernle's Bower MS. *passim*. In the first mentioned inscription the *m* of *siddham* is not much more than a triangle, in the Gupta inscriptions and the Bower MS. *m* is regularly *u*.

[2] In the actually existing signs they appear on the right, because the signs were turned on the change in the direction of the writing.

[3] Dots appear for short horizontal bars also in other cases, *e. g.* in the hyphens at the end of verses, which often look like, and have been misread, as Visargas. *Vice versa* small horizontal strokes are substituted for dots *e. g.* in the letter *I*, which in the inscriptions of the Nasik and Karle caves sometimes consist of three short horizontal bars.

in which *O*,[1] No 6, Col. VI, f—g, has been formed out of *U*, and in the first sign (Col. VI, f), the stroke stands in its [73] original position, because the letter (Jaugada form) has not been turned round. The *AI* (No 16, Col. VI, b, upper row) appears to have been derived from *E* in the same manner, but the letter has been turned from the right to the left. The sounds *u* and *o*, as well as *e* and *ai*, appear to a Hindu and to a Sanskritist closely connected, because in numberless cases *o* is the *Guṇa* or representative of *u* in strong forms, and because *e* and *ai* both appear in the strong forms of roots with *i* and in derivatives from nouns with *i* and *e*. These phonetic or grammatical affinities no doubt influenced the formation of the signs.

Added to signs for consonants, either on the right or across the top, a straight stroke likewise denotes a change of quality viz. that the sign expresses the corresponding sound of a different class or *Varga*. The stroke has its original position in the Bhaṭṭiprolu *ḷ* (No 12, Col. VI), which has not been turned round. It appears on the left in the palatal *ña*,[2] because this has been turned. Its position is again the original one in the guttural *ṅa*, which in the Gayā alphabet and the Kuṣana (see above p. 31) inscriptions is , and in which the foot of the *na* has also been modified. Finally in *ṇa* (No 14, Col. VI, b) the bar goes across the vertical. The peculiarities of the last two letters are probably due to a desire to avoid collisions with *nā*, *ne* and *O*.

Aspiration is expressed by the addition of a curve in the Bhaṭṭiprolu *gha* (No 3, Col. VI), and the ordinary Brāhma signs for *ḍha* (No 4, Col. VI, d), *pha* (No 17, Col. VI) and *cha* (No 18, Col. VI, a—b) are derived in the same manner from *ḍa*, *pa* and *ca*. In the sign for *cha* both ends of the curve have been connected with the vertical line of *ca*. There are numerous instances, like that given in Col. VI, a, in which a difference between the two halves of this letter is clearly discernible, and the one half is angular, the other round. These, I think, are the older forms. The second sign for *cha* (Col. VI, b) which consists

[1] The sign , which is sometimes given for *O* in palaeographic works, does not exist.

[2] See above the remarks under No 14, p. 65.

of a circle bisected by a vertical line is in my opinion cursive.

In the two signs for *bha* (No 2, Col. VI) and for *jha* (No 7, Col. VI) an angle or hook serves the same purpose as the curve of the other four aspirates, and in both cases the original sign is mutilated in order to make the new form less cumbersome. The *ba* has lost its base line and the *ja* its two [74] bars. It seems not improbable, as has already been suggested by others, that the angle or hook of aspiration may be a cursive development from the letter *ha*.

In the lingual *ḷa*, derived from the round *ḍa* (No 4, Col. VI, e) a small semicircle[1] has been added to the foot of the original sign in order to indicate the change of the phonetic value. Here also, I believe, we may recognise the influence of the grammarians or phoneticists. For the sounds *ḍa* and *ḷa* are frequently interchanged in the same word. Thus we find already in the Vedas regularly a *ḷa* for a *ḍa* between two vowels, as in *īḷe* for *īḍe*. In the later Sanskrit and in the Prakrits there are numerous variants like *nāḍī* and *nāḷī*, *nāḍikera* and *nāḷikera* and so forth, where it is often difficult to decide, which is the original form. As the principle, on which the ordinary *ḷa* has been formed, differs from the more general one, applied in the case of the Bhaṭṭiprolu letter, I consider it to be of later origin.

C. *The Medial Vowels.*

Hitherto two systems for the notation of the medial vowels have become known, that of the Edicts and all the later Sanskrit and Prakrit inscriptions and that of Bhaṭṭiprolu. The first, which is by far the older one, shows clearly the influence of the grammarians and their ingenuity. As the vowel, expressed in the beginning of words by the representative of the Semitic *Aleph*, occurs in Sanskrit nearly as frequently as all the

---

[1] Possibly a sign which occurs in Jaugada and in the Pillar Edicts  *i. e.* *ḍa* with a dot a the foot, may have the same value, as it is used in words which have double forms with *ḍa* and *ḷa* or *la* *e. g.* *duḍī* or *duḷī*, *eḍaka* or *eḷaka*, *Coḍā* and *Coḷā*

other vowels taken together,[1] it was not expressed by any sign, but considered to be inherent in all signs for consonants. This device fully agrees with the system of nearly all the phonetic and grammatical treatises, which, as Professor Max Müller has shown so clearly, do not refer to written letters but only to sounds.[2] They almost invariably speak of the *kakāra, gakāra* [75] and so forth. The commentators no doubt are right, when they assert, that the vowel has been added in order to make the pronunciation of the consonants possible, and the vowel *a* was selected for this purpose on account of the frequency of its occurrence. It seems impossible to assume that there is no connexion between the two facts, and, as the grammarians base their theories on spoken words not on written texts, I think that they are the men who also in this case influenced the formation of the Brāhma alphabet.

As regards the other vowels, medial *ā* is expressed by placing to the right of the consonant the same short horizontal stroke,[3] used for the differentiation of the initial *Ā* from *A*, apparently because the other portion, the short *a*, is already contained in the consonant. The remaining ones are expressed by the signs for the initial vowels or by modifications thereof,

---

[1] See Professor Whitney's calculations in his Sanskrit Grammar, p. 73 (second edition).

[2] History Anc. Sansk. Lit., p. 507 ff. This assertion has been hotly contested by Professor Goldstücker in his Introduction to the Mānava Kalpa Sūtra, p. 13 ff. But Professor Kielhorn, who has studied the Vyākaraṇa during so many years, informs me that he does not know of a single passage even in the Bhāṣya, which indicates with certainty, that a written text of Pāṇini's grammar is referred to, or where the technical terms of the grammarians and their theoretical speculations refer to written signs; see also his remarks in Gurupūjākaumudī p. 29 ff. It seems, therefore, to be a fact that the grammatical and phonetic researches were begun either before the introduction of writing or independently of writing, and that even those ancient authors, who like Pāṇini, mention alphabets and clerks, continued to work on in the old manner. I must, however, add that Geheimrath von Böhtlingk dissents and believes that the phrase *yathānyāsam* in the Mahābhāṣya (e. g. I, 22, l. 3) points to a written text.

[3] Originally the stroke, of course, stood on the left, and it is found in this position on the Eraṇ coin, where the letters run from the right to the left, see the Grundriss, Tafel II. 28. I.

placed above or below the consonants. A very clear case is that of the medial *o* in the syllable *ko*,[1] given in two forms under No 6, Col. VI, h—i. If the *k*, *i. e.* the portion of the sign below the second bar, is removed, there remains in the eighth sign a minute initial *o* of the type in Col. VI, f, and in the ninth one of the type in Col. VI, g. Now in the Jaugada version of the Rock Edicts, where the initial *O* has the top bar to the right, the same is invariably the case with the medial *o*. It, therefore, would seem that the writer was perfectly aware of the connection of the two signs. But, in Aśoka's time this [76] feeling was dying out. For in Girnār, where the initial *O* with the top-bar to the left alone is used, the medial *o* is made in both ways, and in the second part of the Delhi Pillar Edict VII, 2, l. 2 we have once the cursive medial *o* in *nigohāni*, where both strokes are placed on the same level above the consonant.

Equally clear is the case of the medial *u*, which is the initial *U*, put below the consonant. This is distinctly recognisable in the sign *dhu* (No 6, Col. VI, b) which occurs repeatedly in the Kālsī version.[2] Cursively it assumes the form, given in Col. VI, c or of ᑭ, with the omission either of the vertical stroke or of the horizontal bar at the end. On the same cursive principle *ū*, which in *kū* etc. retains the shape of *Ū* (Grundriss, I, 11, p. 37), is expressed by two strokes, placed either horizontally at the side of the consonant (No 6, Col. VI, e) or below the consonant, where they frequently form an acute angle but are also placed parallel side by side. These facts seem to indicate that Aśoka's clerks had lost the remembrance of the origin of the signs for medial *u* and *ū*, and that they considered the old forms, which they occasionally used, merely as permissible variants without any special significance. In later inscriptions,[3] however, reminiscences of the origin of the subscript *u* and *ū* are found. Thus in the ancient Śāradā characters of the Baijnāth Praśasti and elsewhere *pū* is expressed by [sign].

As regards the medial *i*, the small angle to the left of the top of the consonant by which it is marked, seems to be

---

[1] Compare also the *go* [sign] in *mago*. Girnār, Ed. I. l. 11, where a distinct *O* stands above *ga*.

[2] *E. g.* in Kālsī, Edict III, l. 8 (twice).

[3] Compare also the Grundriss, *gu* in Taf. VII. 10. 20; *bhu* in Taf. VII. 30. XII; *śu* in Taf. VII. 36. XXI; and *bhū* in Taf. VII. 30. XX—XXI.

the result of a connexion of the three dots of the initial vowel by means of two lines, see the *ki* No 16, Col. VI, d—e, lower row. As long as the Brāhma alphabet was written from the right to the left, the *i*-strokes, as well as all other vowel signs of course stood to the left of the consonant. In the Kālsī version, Ed. XIII, 2, l. 10, there are two signs, at the end of the words *anuvidhiyaṃti* and *anuvidhiyisaṃti*, where the vowel has this position. They look like *A*, because the vowel strokes have been added to the middle of the consonant. A better formed *ti* with the vowel on the left occurs in Allahābād, Ed. I (end), and a similar *hi* on the Sohgaurā copperplate, l. 4. The medial *ī* does not seem to be connected with the initial *Ī*, but to have been formed by the addition of the [77] straight stroke, denoting also in other cases the lengthening of vowels, which for convenience's sake in this case was made vertical. Cursively the angle of medial *i* is converted in Girnar into a shallow curve and medial *ī* is expressed by a curve bisected by a vertical stroke.

The sign for medial *e*, a straight or slanting line to the left of the consonant, I take to be the remnant of a triangular initial *E*, the outlines of which have been indicated by dots in the *ke*, figured under No 16, Col. VI, a, upper row. I may add that in the Edicts forms like λ are occasionally used for *ge*, where the vowel sign seems to consist not of a line, but of a hook put on the top of the letter. Such forms are perhaps ancient survivals, dating from a time when the vowel was represented by an angle, to which the triangle probably was reduced in the first instance. The position of the *e*-stroke is abnormal, as it stands to the left of, or before, the letter, after which it is pronounced. The cause is no doubt, that, if it had been placed to the right, it would have been undistinguishable from medial long *ā*.

In accordance with the form of the initial *AI* consisting of *e* and a horizontal bar to the left of the top, the medial *ai* is expressed by two bars to the left of the consonant, see the syllable *thai* from the Girnār version, given under No 16, Col. VI, c, upper row.

The absence of a medial vowel between two consonants is expressed by the formation of a ligature, in which ordinarily the second consonant or its most essential portion is attached to the foot of the first. In the Girnār and Siddāpur versions however, the ligatures *sṭa, tpa, vya*[1] as well as those containing a *ra,* like *tra, pra* and *vra* show the inverse order and are spelt *ṭsa, pta, yva, rta* and so forth, while all the others like *sta, mha* etc. are formed regularly. Moreover, in the words *brāmhaṇa* (Girnār IV, l. 2) and *drahyitavyaṃ* (Siddāpur, I, l. 9) the first vertical of *ba* and the two vertical strokes of *da* have been converted into wavy *ra*-lines. These irregularities are no [78] doubt due to an artistic feeling and the desire of the clerks to produce regular, shapely signs. The combinations of the consonants with medial vowels furnish analogies. Properly all the vowels ought to stand to the right of the foot of the consonants. If the majority is nevertheless placed at the top, that has been done merely for the sake of convenience. Later inscriptions also furnish a few isolated cases of an inversion of the order of the elements of ligatures. Thus the name of Caṣṭana's father is spelt on the coins *Ysamotika* instead of *Syamotika* and Harṣa's Banskhera Plate of A. D. 628/9 offers *vaṇṇra* for *varṇṇa.*

The cause of the formation of ligatures in order to express the absence of vowels must again be sought for in the influence of the Sanskrit phoneticists on the development of the Brāhma alphabet. The Prātiśākhyas and the later works on phonetics and grammar all use the expression *saṃyuktākṣara* "a conjunct syllable" for groups like *kta, kra* and so forth. The combination of the signs in writing looks very much like a practical illustration of the meaning of the term.

The manner in which the absence of a vowel after a final consonant was probably expressed, has been stated in the remarks on the Anusvāra, above p. 74f.

The Bhaṭṭiprolu system of vowel-notation differs from the ordinary one merely by marking the short *a* by the bar, which denotes *ā* in the Edicts, and the long *ā* by the same bar *plus* a vertical or slanting stroke, hanging down from it, *e. g.* 

[1] At least in *vyaṃjanato,* Ed. III, l. 6. The cases of the passive future participles in *tayva* are doubtful, as they may have been pronounced as they are written, compare Pali *mayham* and so forth. The Siddāpur version has *tavya* in *drahyitavyaṃ.*

na and *nā*. This system, according to which the consonants have no inherent *a*, seems to have been invented in order to avoid the necessity of forming the ligatures, which make the ordinary Brāhma alphabet cumbersome and difficult to read in its later developments, and in order to express final consonants more conveniently. I believe it, therefore, to be of later origin, especially as the other Bhaṭṭiprolu vowel-signs do not differ from the ordinary ones. The invention must, of course, have been made for writing Sanskrit, as the Prakrits have few groups of dissimilar medial consonants and no final ones.

To sum up—the forty four letters[1] of the ordinary Brāhma alphabet, traceable in the oldest inscriptions as well as the variants of the Bhaṭṭiprolu inscrip- [79] tions, contain representatives of, and derivatives from, all the twenty two Semitic characters, viz:—

Semitic letters	Brāhma letters	Derivatives
Aleph	*a* (initial)	*ā* (initial and medial)
Beth	*ba*	*bha*
Gimel	*ga*	*gh* (Bhaṭṭiprolu)
Daleth	*dha*	*da*, *ḍa* { *ḍha* / *ḷa* }
He	*ha*	
Waw	*va*	*u* { *ū* / *o* } (initial and medial)
Zain	*ja*	*jha*
Cheth	*gha*	
Theth	*tha*	*ṭha*, *ṭa*
Yod	*ya*	
Kaph	*ka*	

[1] With respect to the missing *AU* and *(A)ḥ* it may be noted, that the forms of *AU* in the Gupta and Pallava inscriptions, as well as those in the Bower MS., show that it was derived from *O* by the addition of a bar to the right of the vertical. But the medial *au* in the Bharahut Toraṇa inscription (Grundriss, I, 11, Taf. II. 28. XVIII) makes it probable that there was a second form with the additional bar to the left. Regarding the origin of the Visarga, which first occurs in the Kuṣana inscriptions, of the Jihvāmūlīya and Upadhmānīya, first traceable in the Gupta inscriptions, I am not able to suggest anything.

Semitic letters	Brāhma letters	Derivatives
Lamed	*la*	*ḷ* (Bhaṭṭiprolu)
Mem	*ma*	*ṃ* (Anusvāra)
Nun	*na*	*ña* { *ṅa*, *ṇa*
Samech	*ṣ* (Bhaṭṭiprolu)	{ *śa*, *ṣa*
Ain	*e* (initial)	{ *e* (medial) *ai* (init. & med.); *i*, *ī* (initial & medial)
Phe	*pa*	*pha*
Tsade	*ca*	*cha*
Qoph	*kha*	
Resh	*ra*	
Shin	*śa*	
Taw	*ta*	

With the exception of the signs for the sibilants *śa* and *ṣa-sa*, which in consequence of modifications, introduced, it [80] would seem, independently by the Hindus,[1] resemble later Aramaic characters, the Brāhma letters closely agree with or are most easily derivable from the old types of the North-Semitic alphabet. And the Brāhma initial vowels *A* and *E* as well as the consonants *kha, ga, gha, tha, dha, ba* and *va* point to particularly archaic prototypes, while *ha* and *ta* appear to be connected with somewhat modified forms. It would, therefore, seem that the Semitic alphabet became known to the Hindus at a period when the angle of its *Aleph* opened wide and the vertical crossbar protruded about equally on the two sides, when the top of *Beth* was still closed, when *ga* consisted of an angle open below, when *Daleth* had not yet developed a tail, when *Waw* consisted of a semicircular head with a vertical depending from the middle, when *Cheth* had three bars, when *Theth* and *Ain* were quite or nearly circular and *Qoph* had a round head with a vertical hanging down from it, but when the simplified *He* consisting only of three strokes had been developed and the left half of the original crossbar of *Taw* had nearly or quite disappeared.

---

[1] See the remarks made above p. 67 under No 15 and p. 71 under No 21.

According to the dates of the Semitic inscriptions, which can come into question, those of Mesa's stone and the Assyrian weights, this period must fall somewhere between *circiter* 890 and 750 B. C., probably more towards the lower than the remoter of the two limits. Hence the *terminus a quo* for the introduction of the prototypes of the Brāhma letters lies between the beginning of the ninth century and the middle of the eighth, or about 800 B. C. And it seems to me that some further considerations make it probable that their actual importation took place at this early time.

As the Brāhma *ha* goes back to a form of *He,* which is not found in any Phoenician alphabet, but occurs on the Assyrian weights, where also a *Taw* very similar to the Brāhma *ta* is found, the conjecture seems not altogether improbable that the Semitic alphabet may have come to India through Mesopotamia. And it would agree with such an assumption that passages in ancient Indian works prove the early existence of a navigation of the Indian Ocean and the somewhat [81] later occurrence of trading voyages, undertaken by Hindu merchants to the shores of the Persian Gulf and its rivers.

The now well known Bāveru Jātaka,[1] to which Professor Minayeff first drew attention, narrates that Hindu merchants exported peacocks to Bāveru. The identification of Bāveru with Babiru or Babylon is not doubtful, and according to what has been said, above p. 16 ff., regarding the age of the materials of the Jātakas, the story indicates that the Vāṇiās of Western India undertook trading voyages to the shores of the Persian Gulf and of its rivers in the fifth, perhaps even in the sixth century B. C., just as in our days. This trade very probably existed already in much earlier times. For the Jātakas contain several other stories, describing voyages to distant lands and perilous adventures by sea, in which the names of the very ancient Western ports of Śūrpāraka-Supārā and Bharukacha-Broach are occasionally mentioned. References to sea-voyages are also found in two of the most ancient Dhar-

---

[1] No 339, see Fausböll, Jātakas, Vol. III, p. 126 ff. It has been translated by Professor Rhys Davids in the Babylonian and Oriental Record, Vol. III, p. 7 ff.

masūtras. Baudhāyana,[1] Dh. S. II, 2, 2, forbids them to the orthodox Brahmans and prescribes a severe penance for a transgression of the prohibition. But he admits, Dh. S. I, 2, 4, that such transgressions were common among the "Northerners", or strictly speaking, the Aryans living north of the author's home, the Dravidian districts. The other forbidden practices, mentioned in the same Sūtra as customary among the Northerners, such as the traffic in wool and in animals with two rows of teeth, (horses, mules, etc.), leave no doubt that the inhabitants of Western and Northwestern India are meant. It follows as a matter of course that their trade was carried on with Western Asia. The same author, Dh. Ś. I. 18. 14 and Gautama, X. 33 fix also the duties, payable by shipowners to the king. Even from still earlier times there is the story of a shipwreck, the scene of which must have been the Indian [82] Ocean. Numerous hymns of the Ṛgveda mention the mighty deed of the twin brethren, the Aśvins, who saved Bhujyu, the son of Tugra, from the sea, "where, as one account says,[2] there is no support, no rest for the foot or the hand, after he had ascended the hundred-oared galley," of the two deities.

The later Vedic literature contains also a few evidently Semitic legends, among which that of the Deluge and Manu's preservation in a ship, built by the advice of a miraculous fish, is the most noteworthy,[3] and it is possible, that they may have been brought over from Mesopotamia by the early Indian navigators and traders. But this is of course a mere pos-

---

[1] Sacred Books of the East, Vol. XIV, pp. 146, 200, 217. Later Smṛtis *e. g.* Manu VIII, 157, give rules regarding marine insurance and other matters referring to sea-borne trade. Moreover, Manu III, 156 declares a Brahman, who has gone to sea, to be unworthy of entertainment at a Śrāddha.

[2] Ṛ. V. I, 116. 5, see also the larger St. Petersburg Dictionary *sub voce* Bhujyu, and Prof. Oldenberg, Vedische Religion, p. 214. I quite agree with Professor Oldenberg regarding the interpretation of the myth, but I would not venture to infer from the deeds of the Aśvins and of their Greek representatives, the Dioskouroi, that the Indo-European race originally dwelt near the sea.

[3] I am glad to see that Professor Oldenberg, Vedische Religion, p. 276, also declares this myth to be borrowed from a Semitic source, in spite of Prof. M. Müller's and Prof. Lindner's attempts to make it an Indo-Aryan invention.

sibility, and other explanations of their occurrence in the Brahmanical literature may be and have been, suggested. The passages, adduced above, are however sufficient to prove that the Indo-Aryans began to navigate the Indian Ocean in very remote times, and it is, therefore, quite imaginable that they themselves imported the Semitic letters from Mesopotamia.[1]

Between this importation and the complete elaboration of the Brāhma alphabet there lay, however, in all probability a prolonged period. This, I think, appears from the following considerations. One of the undeniable results of the preceding enquiry is that the Brāhma alphabet must be considered the work of Brahmans, acquainted with phonetic and grammatical theories. The Pandit's hand is clearly visible in the arrangement of the letters, used by Aśoka's masons at Mahābodhi Gayā, according to their organic value as vowels, diphthongs, nasalised vowel, vowel with the spirant, gutturals, palatals and linguals. And it is also visible at a much earlier stage, in the very formation of the alphabet. Nobody but a [83] grammarian or phoneticist would have thought of deriving five nasals, one for each class of the Indian consonants, from the two Semitic prototypes and of inventing in addition a sign to denote the nasalisation of vowels, the Anusvāra, or of forming two spirants, *ha* and the Visarga. Nobody but a Sanskrit grammarian would express the initial *U* by half the sign for *va*,[2] and the phonetically very different, but etymologically allied *ṣa* and *sa* by modifications of one sign, or derive the initial *O* from *U*, *I* from *E*[3] and *ḷa* from *ḍa*.[4] And only a grammarian would invent the peculiar system of notation for medial vowels, which throughout marks the distinction between short and long ones[5] omits the short *a*, and expresses the long *ā* by adding to the consonants the mark, used for differentiating *Ā* from *A*, and the remaining medial vowels by combinations of the initial vowel-

[1] Compare the case of the Tibetan alphabet, the elements of which the Tibetan Thon-mi or Sambhoṭa is said to have imported from Magadha between A. D. 630—660, Jour. As. Soc. Bengal, vol. LVII, p. 41 f.

[2] See above p. 74.

[3] See above p. 66 f.

[4] See above p. 77.

[5] See Wackernagel, Altindische Grammatik, vol. I, p. LVII, Note 3.

signs, or of modifications thereof, with the consonants. This is so complicated and so highly artificial that only a Brahman's or Pandit's ingenuity can have worked it out.

There are also very good reasons for alleging that an Indian alphabet, elaborated by traders or other men of business, clerks and accountants, would never have possessed a single medial vowel. For until a very recent period, within the last fifty years, the Indian traders never used any medial vowels in their books or in their correspondence. Almost every child in Gujarāt knows the story of the letter,[1] sent by a Vāṇio to his relatives, which caused great grief and lamentation owing to the want of the vowel signs. The letter, it is said, contained the following passage: कक अजमर गय अन कक कट छ ॥ On seeing it, the recipients at once began to lament loudly. They interpreted it to mean:—काको आज मरी गयो अने काकी कूटे छे "Uncle died today and aunt beats her breast." A sympathising neighbour inquired for the cause of the wailing. On being shown the letter, he remarked that the outside did not bear the usual superscription of announcements of deaths, viz. "Strip and [84] read",[2] and he suggested that the missive might be read:—काको अजमीर गयो अने काकी कोट छे "Uncle has gone to Ajmīr and aunt is at Koṭ." On further enquiry this proved to be correct.

The progress of vernacular education and the action of the English lawcourts and of the native princes has of late changed these habits of the mercantile classes. As the law courts refuse to take ledgers written without vowel-signs as legal evidence, as the native princes follow suit,[3] and as the schools now teach composition, the Vāṇiās and accountants write

[1] The story is a regular Indian "Joe Miller", and is commonly told by the masters to the schoolboys. Dr. G. A. Grierson informs me that a similar story is current in the Bengal Presidency.

[2] A Hindu becomes impure on hearing of the death of a relative and is obliged to throw away the clothes, which he wears when the news of such an event comes. In order to obviate unnecessary loss, the announcements of deaths bear on the outside the words, given above.

[3] In 1875 Mahārāja Raṇbīrsingh of Kaśmīr told me that he had weaned his clerks from the bad habit of writing their Ṭakkarī or Dogrā characters without vowels by refusing to pass accounts written in this manner.

at present more frequently in the same manner as the Brahmans do and have done always and almost without exception.[1]

With such propensities prevailing among the business people of modern times, it is difficult to believe that those belonging to a very remote antiquity would have acted differently and would have framed for their writing a vowel-system which their descendants discarded. Nevertheless—though the Brahman schoolmen undoubtedly have framed the Brāhma alphabet,—the introduction of its elements, the Semitic signs, into India is presumably due to the merchant class.[2] For the Vāṇiās naturally came most into contact with foreign nations. Moreover, they were the men who most urgently wanted a means for perpetuating the record of their daily transactions, while the Brahmans possessed since very early times the system of oral instruction for preserving their literary composi-
[85] tions and for teaching them to their pupils, to which they have always adhered. Traces of the existence of this system are found, as Professor Max Müller has already pointed out, even in the Ṛgveda, in the famous Frog-hymn, Ṛ.V., VII, 103, 5, where it is said of the bull-frogs, that the one imitates the cry of the other, "just as a pupil repeats the words of his teacher". Its full development, which is found in the later Vedic works, both the Brāhmaṇas and the Vedāṅgas and has been described repeatedly,[3] must certainly be as early as the period when the Semitic letters can have been imported, or even more ancient. With this system the Brahmans cannot have felt the necessity for writing so strongly as the men of business, and it is also for this reason improbable that they should have been the first Hindus who practised writing. Nay,

---

[1] I have seen one Gujarātī inscription without vowels, which *may* be due to a Brahman. It is incised on the right hand gate post of the temple of Dharaṇīdhar at Dehemā in Northwestern Gujarat and omitting the date, runs thus: तरख न फज आव न वव न रव हर ॥ Its meaning was interpreted to me, as follows: तुरखनी फोज आवी ने वावनो राओ हार्यो "The Musalman army came and the Rāo of Vāv was defeated."

[2] See also Westergaard, Zwei Abhandlungen, p. 37 f.

[3] M. Müller, History of Ancient Sanskrit Literature, p. 503 ff., compare also A. Weber, Indische Studien, X, p. 128 ff.

it may be even doubted whether they cared to undertake the adaptation of the foreign invention very soon after it had become known to the mercantile class.

Further, when they undertook it, the evolution of the 46 signs of the Brāhmī lipi from the 22 Semitic characters cannot have been accomplished very quickly. The evidence of the Bhaṭṭiprolu alphabet shows that in the case of several letters more attempts than one were made, and the alphabet of the Edicts, the ordinary Brāhmī lipi, likewise bears witness that the signs were invented gradually. As has been pointed out above, the dental *dha* yielded, by a slight transposition of one of its lines, the dental *da,* from this the lingual *ḍa* was derived by the omission of the lower vertical stroke, and from the lingual *ḍa* came, by the addition of a curve, the lingual *ḍha,* as well as, by the addition of the semicircle, the lingual *ḷa.* The series of the derivatives from *va,* from the dental *tha,* the dental *na,* the Bhaṭṭiprolu *ṣ* and from the initial *E* are similarly complicated. It is incredible that in these cases the whole series of derivatives should have been invented at one time or even in quick succession, though no doubt the Brahmans had their system of phonetics, based on spoken works, to guide them and to help them on.

[86] It would thus seem that a not inconsiderable interval must lie between the first importation of the Semitic letters and the complete elaboration of the Brāhma alphabet. First the imported characters remained in the hands of the traders and the men of business, during which period, as perhaps may be inferred from the treatment of the Arabic letters during the Mahommedan period, none or very slight modifications were introduced. Next came the transference of the foreign invention to the Brahmans and finally its adaptation to the wants of the Sanskrit language.

These considerations certainly show that the introduction of the Semitic letters must fall centuries before the period when the Brāhma alphabet was in general use, *i. e.* 500 B. C. or thereabouts. And they thus confirm the approximate date, deduced above from the age of the Semitic signs, which appear to have been the prototypes of the Indian modifications. This date, I repeat, is merely approximate and I may add, provisional. New finds of ancient Semitic or Indian inscriptions may, and very likely will, alter it. And I should not be surprised, if such discoveries forced us to put the *terminus a quo* for the introduction of the Semitic characters into India earlier than is advisable on the evidence, available at present.

Finally, the fact that the Brâhma alphabet is the work of the Brahmans has also, it seems to me, a certain bearing on the vexed question whether in ancient times writing was used for literary purposes. I believe that it enables us to answer this question in the affirmative, of course with certain reservations. For the Brahmans, though often considered mere dreamers, are in reality very practical people, who, as far as my observation goes, do not take and never have taken trouble with anything that does not serve their purposes. As they adapted the Semitic letters to the wants of their sacred language in a very thorough manner, I consider it certain that they also utilised their invention at once for their special aims, the cultivation of learning, and that they committed at least their scientific compositions to writing. It is not necessary, nor even probable, that in early times the MSS. were used otherwise than *esoterically*, as auxiliaries for composition and for the preservation of the texts, much in the manner suggested by Geheimrath von Böhtlingk, Professor Whitney and Dr. Burnell.[1]

Their Mantras and other sacred compositions may have remained unwritten somewhat longer. That is no more than might be expected, as the Brahmans had a great interest in [87] keeping their "great medicine" secret. And there are also several indications to this effect, such as the imprecations against copyists of the Veda and the general feeling, even among the heterodox sectarians, that sacred books ought to be preserved only orally.

The Southern Bauddhas and the Jainas give expression to this feeling by asserting that their sacred books were written only many centuries after their composition. But it may be doubted, whether their dates are always quite correct. The occurrence of a *peṭaki* (literally "a Piṭaka-possessor") a monk who knows one or more Piṭakas (see above p. 18), certainly proves that the

[1] See Elements of South-Indian Palaeography, p. 10 and compare also the Grundriss, I, 11, p. 3 f.

Buddhist scriptures were written, when the Bharahut Stūpa was built. *Piṭaka* is only 'a basket' or 'a box' and corresponds to the modern *ḍābaḍo* of cardboard or wood in which the Jainas usually keep the MSS. of their parish libraries. As soon as the Buddhists divided their scriptures into Piṭakas,[1] they must of course have been written. If, as I believe, the inscription of the *peṭaki,* which shows the same characters as the Edicts, belongs approximately to the same time as the latter, the traditional date of the Ceylonese Buddhists, who say that their Canon was first committed to writing about 88 B. C., must be considerably wrong. The oldest MSS., actually found, are probably the birch bark leaves, inscribed with Kharoṣṭhī letters, from the topes of the Panjab.[3] Next comes the Bower MSS. with the characters of the oldest Gupta inscriptions, then follow the Horiuzi palmleaf, the Bakhshāli MS., the Cambridge Collection from Nepal and the Bombay Collections of Jaina MSS. Older documents than are accessible at present, both on birchbark or palmleaves and on stone or metal, will no doubt be found, as soon as the old historical sites of India are excavated in a thorough and rational manner.

---

[1] The term *piṭaka* occurs in one of the latest portions of the Vinaya, the Parivāra, I, 1 (Oldenberg Vinaya piṭaka, vol. V, p. 3), where also a *tipeṭakī* is mentioned.

[2] Though often appealed to in proof of the late use of writing for literary purposes (see e. g. Sacred Books of the East, vol. XIII, p. XXXV ff.), this assertion of the Dīpavaṃsa and Mahāvaṃsa is, I fear, not worth much more than the contradictory story of the Chinese Buddhists. The Chinese boldly assert that the Canon was written on palm leaves immediately after Buddha's death (Grundriss, I, 11, p. 89) and that in A. D. 489 a MS. of the Vinaya was extant, which bore 975 dots, marking the number of the readings at the annual Pavāraṇā since the time of Upāli, who is said to have entered the first dot (Jour. R. As. Soc., 1896, p. 436 f.). Like similar, certainly incorrect, stories of the Brahmans and others regarding their scriptures, the tradition of the two Pali chronicles may be taken merely as the product of the well founded belief that the Buddhists, imitating the Brahmans, preserved their scriptures orally for a prolonged period. But even if it is considered to be historical, it refers only to Ceylon not to India.

[3] One small fragment with the letters *mi*, *dha* and *ya* (?) is figured in H. H. Wilson's Ariana Antiqua, Plate III, No 11.

Appendix I.

The Origin of the Kharoṣṭhī Alphabet.

[44][1] Though the origin of the Kharoṣṭhī alphabet is much easier to explain than the derivation of the Brāhmī and though the general lines for the enquiry have already been settled by others, yet a somewhat fuller review of the whole question, than the narrow compass of my *Grundriss der indischen Palaeographie* permits, will perhaps not be superfluous. The very considerable progress, which has been achieved, is chiefly due to the discussions of the Kharoṣṭhī by Mr. E. Thomas in his edition of *Prinsep's Essays,* vol. II, p. 147 ff., by Dr. Isaac Taylor in *The Alphabet,* vol. II, p. 256 ff., and by Sir A. Cunningham, who has also settled the value of many of its signs, in his book on *The Coins of Ancient India*, p. 31 ff.

Sir A. Cunningham's remarks refer to the first point which requires consideration in all questions of this kind, viz. the true character of the script, the origin of which is to be determined. He has emphatically recalled to the memory of the palaeographists that the Kharoṣṭhī is an Indian alphabet, and by an ingenious utilisation of his finds of ancient coins in the ruins of Taxila he has shown that the Kharoṣṭhī held always, during the whole period for which epigraphic evidence is available, only a secondary position by the side of the Brāhma alphabet even in Northwestern India. It is rather curious that the reminder regarding the essentially Indian character of the alphabet should have been necessary, as even a superficial

[1] The bracketed figures refer to the pages of the first edition of this article in the Wiener Zeitschrift für die Kunde des Morgenlandes, (Vienna Oriental Journal) vol. IX.

considera- [45] tion of its letters teaches that lesson. Its full system of palatals and linguals cannot be designed for any other language than Sanskrit or an ancient Prakrit, the only forms of speech which possess five sounds of each of the two classes mentioned. If this has been sometimes forgotten and even Bactria has been considered as the cradle of the Kharoṣṭhī, the cause is no doubt the loose way in which it used to be called the "Bactrian, Bactro-Pali or Indo-Bactrian" alphabet, which appellations are due to its occurrence on the coins of Greek kings, who, originally ruling over Bactria, conquered portions of Northwestern India. Sir A. Cunningham very properly points out, op. cit., p. 35, that not a single Kharoṣṭhī inscription has been found north of the Hindu Kush and that in Bactria a different alphabet seems to have been used. He further proposes to substitute for "Indo-Bactrian" the Indian term "Gandharian", which would have been suitable in every way, if in the mean time the old Indian name had not been found. The districts, in which the largest number of Kharoṣṭhī inscriptions have been found, are situated roughly speaking between 69°—73°, 30′ E. L. and 33°—35° N. L., while single inscriptions have turned up southwest near Multan, south at Mathurā and east at Kangra, and single letters or single words even at Bharahut, in Ujjain and in Maisur. This tract, to which the Kharoṣṭhī inscriptions of the third century B. C. are exclusively confined, corresponds to the Gandhāra country of ancient India, the chief towns of which were Puṣkalāvatī-Hashtnagar to the west of the Indus and Taxila or Shah Deri to the east of the river. And it is here, of course, that the Kharoṣṭhī alphabet must have originated.

In addition, Sir A. Cunningham has shown that the Kharoṣṭhī held always a secondary position and was used even in the earliest times side by side with the Brāhmī. This is proved by the evidence of his coins from Taxila, several of which bear only Brāhma inscriptions or Kharoṣṭhī and Brāhma inscriptions, with letters of the type of Aśoka's Edicts. The analysis of the legends, which I have given ante p. 48f., shows that those of four types have been issued by traders' guilds and that one is probably a tribal [46] coin, belonging to a subdivision of the Aśvakas or Assakenoi, who occupied portions of the western bank of the Indus at the time of Alexander's invasion. This result considerably strengthens Sir A. Cunningham's position, as it indicates a popular use of the Brāhma alphabet in the very home of the Kharoṣṭhī.

The next step which is required, is to find the class of alphabets, to which the prototypes of the Kharoṣṭhī belonged. This problem is settled, as Mr. Thomas has first pointed out, by the close resemblance of the signs for *na, ba, va* and *ra* to, or identity with, the *Nun, Beth, Waw* and *Resh* of the transitional Aramaic alphabet, and requires no further discussion.

Then comes the question, how the Hindus of Northwestern India can have become acquainted with the Aramaic characters and which circumstances may have induced them to utilise these signs for the formation of a new alphabet. Dr. Taylor, *The Alphabet,* vol. II, p. 261f., answers this by the suggestion that the Akhaemenian conquest of Northwestern India, which occurred not very long before B. C. 500 and led to a prolonged occupation, probably carried the Aramaic or, as he calls it, the Iranian, Persian or Bactrian, alphabet into the Panjab and caused its naturalisation in that province. Though it seems to me, just as to Sir A. Cunningham, impossible to accept Dr. Taylor's reasoning in all its details, I believe with Sir A. Cunningham that he has found the true solution of this part of the problem. For even if the doubtful and often disputed[1] conquest of western Gandhāra by Cyrus about B. C. 530 and the equally doubtful and disputed continuance of its occupation during the reign of Cambyses were historical, the introduction of the Aramaean letters into the Indian province could only date from the reign of Darius. According to all accounts Darius first organised the administration of the Akhaemenian empire and first sent Satraps with their staff of subordinate officials into the provinces. It is obvious that only such an administrative organisation could cause the spread of the official alphabet in the remoter portions of the empire.

One argument in his favour is the occurrence of the Old Persian word *dipi* "writing, edict" in the Northwestern versions

[1] Disputed e. g. by Lassen, Niese, J. Oppert and G. Rawlinson, assumed to be historical by Droysen, Dunker and others.

of the Edicts and of its derivatives *dipati* "he writes" and *dipapati* "he causes to write", which are not found in any other Indian language. *Dipi* is undoubtedly as Dr. Taylor himself has stated an Old Persian loanword, and all the three words mentioned point to a Persian influence, dating from the Akhaemenian period. And the Sanskrit and Pali *lipi* or *libi* "writing, written document", which does not occur in the Vedic and Epic literature, nor in the ancient works of the Buddhist Canon of Ceylon, but appears first in Sūtras of Pāṇini, a native of Gandhāra (traditional date *circiter* 350 B. C.), furnishes the same [47] indication, since in all probability, as Dr. Burnell conjectured, it is a corruption of *dipi*, favoured by a fancied connexion with the verb *lip, limpati* "he smears" (see above, 21 f.). Equally valuable is a second point, the fact that the territory of the Kharoṣṭhī corresponds very closely with the extent of the portion of India, presumably held by the Persians. Dr. Taylor and Sir A. Cunningham very justly lay stress on the statement of Herodotus (III, 94, 96) who asserts that the Persian satrapy of India paid a tribute of 360 talents of gold dust. They naturally infer that the Indian possessions of the Akhaemenians must have been of considerable extent, as well as that they must have included the greater portion of the Panjab.

But there remain still two gaps which must needs be filled up. The Akhaemenian theory requires it to be shown that the ancient Persians actually used the Aramaic letters and that peculiar circumstances existed which compelled the Hindus to use these letters. The second point is at present particularly important, because the literary evidence regarding the use of writing in India[1] (with which the epigraphic evidence fully agrees) proves that the Hindus were by no means unlettered in the fifth and sixth centuries B. C., but possessed and extensively used an alphabet, which probably was a form of the Brāhmī *lipi*. As long as it was possible to maintain that the Hindus became acquainted with the art of writing not earlier than 400 B. C., it was, of course, easy to understand, that the use of the Aramaic letters by the conquerors of Northwestern India should have acted as a natural incentive for their Hindu

[1] Ante p. 5ff.

subjects to form out of these characters an alphabet suited for their own language. But the case becomes different, if it must be admitted that the Hindus possessed already a script of their own before the Persian conquest. With this admission it becomes neccessary to show that there were special circumstances which forced them to use the alphabet of their conquerors.

Both the points just discussed are explained, it seems to me, by certain discoveries, made of late years in Semitic palaeography. M. Clermont-Ganneau's important articles in the *Revue archéologique* [48] of 1878 and 1879 have shown that the Aramaic language and writing, which already in the times of the Assyrian empire occur in contracts and on the official standard weights, were frequently employed for official correspondence, accounts and other official purposes during the rule of the Akhaemenian kings in many different provinces of their empire. Egypt has furnished Aramaic inscriptions on stones and potsherds as well as Aramaic Papyri, addressed to Persian governors; in western Asia and in Arabia both inscriptions and numerous Satrap coins with Aramaic legends have been found, and even Persia has yielded an Aramaic inscription (of which unfortunately no trustworthy facsimile exists) at Senq-Qaleh, midway between Tabriz and Teheran.[1] And, I may add, there is also a scrap of literary evidence to the same effect. A statement in the Book of Ezra IV. 7, points to the conclusion that the Aramaic language and writing was well-known in the Imperial *chancellerie* at Susa. For it is said that a letter, addressed by the Samaritans to Artaxerxes, "was written", as the Revised Version of the Bible has it, "in the Syrian *(character)* and in the Syrian tongue". The Samaritans would hardly have adopted the "Arāmīt" in addressing their liege lord, if it had not been commonly used in official correspondence, sent out from, or into, the Imperial Secretariat.[2]

---

[1] See Ph. Berger, *Histoire de l'Écriture dans l'Antiquité*, p. 218 ff., where M. Berger pertinently remarks with respect to the last inscription, that it puts us on the road to India.

[2] As Prof. Euting kindly points out to me, a similar inference has already been drawn from the above passage by the authors of the *Kurzgef. Commentar z. d. heil. Schriften d. N. u. A. Test.*, hg. v. H. Strack und O. Zöckler; Alt. Test., Abth. 8, p. 159.

The custom itself, no doubt, has to be explained by a strong infusion of Aramaeans, or of men trained in the learning of the Aramaeans, in the lower grades of the Persian Civil Service, among the scribes, accountants, treasurers and mint-masters, and this is no more than might be expected, when a race like the Persian suddenly comes into the possession of a very large empire and becomes the heir of an older civilisation.

Under these circumstances it appears natural to assume that the Persian Satraps carried with them also into India their staff of [49] subordinates, who were accustomed to the use of the Aramaean letters and language. And this would fully explain, how the Hindus of the Indo-Persian provinces were driven to utilise the characters, commonly employed by the scribes and accountants of their conquerors, though they already possessed a script of their own. The Kharoṣṭhī alphabet would appear to be the result of the intercourse between the offices of the Satraps and of the native authorities, the Indian chiefs and the heads of towns and villages, whom, as the accounts of the state of the Panjab at the time of Alexander's invasion show, the Persians left in possession in consideration of the payment of their tribute. The Hindus probably used at first the pure Aramaic characters, just as in much later times they adopted the Arabic writing for a number of their dialects, and they introduced in the course of time the modifications, observable in the Kharoṣṭhī alphabet, for which process the additions to the Arabic alphabet, employed for writing Hindī, furnish an analogy, perhaps not perfect but nevertheless worthy of notice.

In support of these conjectural combinations three further points may be adduced. First, the Kharoṣṭhī alphabet is not a Pandit's, but a clerk's, alphabet. This appears to me evident from the cursive appearance of the signs, which has been frequently noticed by others, from its (according to Indian views) imperfect vowel-system, which includes no long vowels, from the employment of the Anusvāra for the notation of all nasals before consonants and from the almost constant substitution of single consonants for double ones. The expression of all long vowels by separate signs, which occurs in no other ancient alphabet but the Brāhmī lipi, was no doubt natural and desirable for the phoneticists or grammarians, who developed that alphabet.[1] But it is a useless encumbrance for men of business, whose aim is rather the expeditious despatch of work than philological or phonetic accuracy. Hence, even the Indian clerks and men of business using the Brāhmī, have never paid much attention to their correct use, though they were in- [50] structed by Brahmans in the principles of their peculiar alphabet.[2] If, therefore, these signs, which have only a value for schoolmen, do not occur in the Kharoṣṭhī, the natural inference is that this alphabet was framed by persons who paid regard only to the requirements of ordinary life. The other two peculiarities mentioned, the substitution of the Anusvāra for all nasals, standing before consonants, and the substitution of *ka* for *kka*, of *ta* for *tta* and so forth and of *kha* for *kkha*, of *dha* for *ddha* and so forth, are clearly the devices of clerks, who wished to get quickly through their work. If thus the Kharoṣṭhī appears to be an alphabet, framed with particular regard to the wants of clerks, that agrees with and confirms the assumption, put forward above, according to which it arose out of the official intercourse between the scribes of the Satraps and those of the native chiefs or other authorities.

More important, however, is the second point, which is intimately connected with the details of the derivation of the Kharoṣṭhī. The originals of the Kharoṣṭhī letters are, it seems to me, to be found in the Aramaic inscriptions, incised during the rule of the earlier Akhaemenian kings. The whole *ductus* of the Kharoṣṭhī with its long verticals or slanting downstrokes is that of the Saqqārah inscription of 482 B. C. and the probably contemporaneous larger Teima inscription, which Professor Euting assigns to *circiter* 500 B. C. It is also in these inscriptions that most of the forms occur, which apparently have served as models for the corresponding letters of the Kharoṣṭhī. One or perhaps two seem to rest on forms found in the somewhat later Lesser Teima, Serapeum and Stele Vaticana inscriptions, while three are connected with older letters on the Assyrian Weights and the Seals and Gems from Babylon.

---

[1] Ante p. 86f.

[2] Ante p. 43f., note 3.

The accompanying Comparative Table, Plate II,[1] illustrates the details of the derivation, as I understand it. Cols. I and II have been reproduced by photozincography from Professor Euting's Tabula Scripturae [51] Aramaicae, Argentorati 1892, and give the twenty Aramaic signs, which, as I believe, have been utilised by the Hindus, *Theth* and *Ain* being rejected by them.[2] In Col. I the fat signs belong to the Teima inscription (Euting, Col. 9) with the exception of No 1, I, b and No 9, I, b—c, which come from the Stele Vaticana (Euting, Col. 12). The thin signs have been taken from the Sâqqârah inscription (Euting, Col. 11) with the exception of No 4, I, a; No 9, I, a; No 10, I, b and No 20, I, a, which are from the Assyrian Weights and the Babylonian Seals and Gems (Euting, Cols. 6, 8), as well as of No 17, I, a—b, which are from the Serapeum inscription (Euting, Col. 12), and of No 10, I, a, which Professor Euting has kindly added on once more looking over the Babylonian Aramaic inscriptions.[3]

The signs of Col. II have all been taken from Professor Euting's Cols. 14—17, and represent the chief types on the Aramaic Papyri, which M. J. Halévy[4] and others believe to be the prototypes of the Kharoṣṭhī. They have been given in my Table chiefly in order to show that they are not suited for the derivation. Col. III gives the oldest forms of the borrowed Kharoṣṭhī letters according to Tafel I of my *Grundriss der Indischen Paläographie*, and Col. IV with the signs, which I consider to be derivatives invented by the Hindus, comes from the same source.

---

[1] Arranged by Dr. W. Cartellieri and etched by Messrs. Angerer & Göschl of Vienna.

[2] According to Dr. Taylor these two characters are also, reflected in the Kharoṣṭhī. But the sign opposite *Theth* in his Table, *The Alphabet*, vol. II, p. 236, is a late *vra*, and *Ain*, cannot be *O*, as he doubtfully suggests. M. Halévy identifies *Theth* with the letter, which used to be read *tha*, but is in reality *ṭha* and a derivative from *ṭa*, see below.

[3] In this as well as in other respects I have to acknowledge Professor Euting's kind assistance, who sacrificed a good deal of time in order to verify the Semitic signs, which I had selected for comparison, in the Plates of the Corp. Inscr. Sem. and carefully went with me through my Table during a personal interview in Strassburg.

[4] *Journ. Asiatique* 1885, p. 251 ff.

Before I proceed to give my remarks on the details of the derivation, I will restate the general principles which have to be kept in mind for this and all other similar researches.

[52] (1) The oldest actually occurring signs of the alphabet to be derived (in this case the Kharoṣṭhī) have to be compared with the supposed prototypes (in this case actually occurring Aramaic signs) of the same period (in this case of ca. 500—400 B. C.).

(2) Only such irregular equations of signs are admissible as can be supported by analogies from other cases, where nations are known to have borrowed foreign alphabets. Thus it is not permissible to identify the Kharoṣṭhī sign for *ja* with the Aramaic *ga* on account of a rather remote resemblance between what the modern researches have shown to be a secondary form of the Kharoṣṭhī palatal media and the guttural media of the Aramaeans.

(3) The comparison must show that there are fixed principles of derivation.

The latter are given chiefly by the unmistakable tendencies underlying the formation of the Kharoṣṭhī signs,

(1) A very decided predilection for forms, consisting of long vertical or slanting lines with appendages added do the upper portion,

(2) An antipathy against such with appendages at the foot of the verticals, which in no case allows a letter to consist of a vertical with an appendage at the foot alone;

(3) An aversion against heads of letters, consisting of more than two lines rising upwards, as well as against top lines encumbered with transverse or pendant strokes.

These tendencies required two Aramaic letters, *Lamed,* (No 11, I and III) and *Shin* (No 19, I and III) to be turned topsy-turvy, and caused in the Shin the development of a long vertical out of the short central stroke, as well as mutilations of some other signs. And it would seem that the aversion against appendages at the foot is probably due to the desire to keep the lower ends of the *mātṛkās* free for the addition of the medial *u,* the Anusvāra and the *ra*-strokes which are ordinarily added here, while the top lines were kept free from transverse or pendant lines on account of the signs for medial *i, e* and *o*. Some other changes, such as turnings from the right to the left, have been made in order to avoid collisions with other signs, while again other modifi- [53] cations are purely cursive or due to considerations of convenience in writing.

As regards the details, I have to offer the following remarks regarding the Borrowed Signs.

No 1. The identity of *A* with *Aleph* is evident enough (Thomas, Taylor, Halévy). The long stretched shape of the Kharoṣṭhī letter, which leans to the right, makes it in my opinion more probable that it is a simplification of a sign like that from the Saqqārah inscription in Col. I, a, than that it should be connected with the diminutive letters in Col. I, b and in Col. II, which are inclined the other way.

No 2. *Ba* is, of course, a slightly modified form of the *Beth* in Col. I, a—b (Thomas, Taylor and Halévy). The upward bulge next to the vertical has been introduced in order to make the letter with one stroke of the pen, and the bent line at the foot is represented by a prolongation of the vertical in accordance with the principle stated above. The *Beth* of the Papyri (when cursive forms are used as in Col. II, b—c and in Professor Euting's Col. 15 b—c, 16 b—d) is more advanced than the Kharoṣṭhī *ba*.

No 3. The identity of *ga* (Col. III) with *Gimel* (Cols. I and II) has been recognised by Dr. Taylor alone. The loop on the right has been caused by the desire to make the letter with one stroke of the pen. It may be pointed out as an analogy that in the late Kharoṣṭhī of the first and second centuries A. D. cursive loops are common in ligatures with *ra* and *ya* and that there is a looped *ja*, exactly resembling a *ga*, on the Bimāran vase in the word *Muṃjavata*. The Aramaic prototype may possibly have been set up straighter than the forms given in Cols. I and II, and it may be noted that such forms occur already on the Mesa stone and in other old inscriptions, see Euting, Cols. 1 and 3.

No 4. *Da* (Col. III) comes, as has been asserted by all my predecessors, from a *Daleth* like that in Col. I, a, which is found, as Professor Euting informs me, already on an Assyrian Weight of *circiter* 600 B. C. The cursive simplification of this letter was therefore ancient in Mesopotamia. It re-occurs in the Papyri, with a slight [54] modification, compare especially Euting, Col. 14 b. The hook at the foot of the *da,* (Col. III, b), which occurs twice in the Aśoka Edicts and survives in the later inscriptions, seems to have been added in order to distinguish the letter from *na* (No 13, III, a).

No 5. The identity of *ha* (Col. III) with *He* has not been recognised hitherto. But it seems to me derived from a round *He,* like the Teima form in Col. I, a, with the transposition of the central vertical to the lower right end of the curve, which is particularly clear in the letter, given in Col. III, b, a not uncommon form in the Aśoka Edicts. A similar transposition of an inconvenient pendant, due to the consideration for the medial *i, e* and *o,* will be noticed below under No 17. The *He* of the Papyri, though not rarely round at the top, shows nearly always a continuation of the central bar on the outside of the topline, and hence is less suitable for comparison.

No 6. *Va* has preserved, as all previous writers have acknowledged, exactly the form of the *Waw* in the Teima inscription, which re-occurs on various later documents as the Ostraka from Elephantine and the Cilician Satrap coins, and which is foreshadowed by the letter of the ancient Assyrian Weights in Euting's Tabula Col. 6. The Papyri again offer a more advanced round form, which is common in the Kharoṣṭhī inscriptions, incised during the first and second centuries of our era.

No 7. Dr. Taylor alone derives *ja* (Col. III, a—b) from *Zain,* apparently relying on the similar Pehlevi letter. The form in Col. III, a, which is found repeatedly[1] in the Mansehra version and survives in the legends of the Indo-Grecian and Śaka coins, is, however, without doubt the oldest, and derived from a *Zain,* like those of the Teima inscription (Col. I, a—b) in which the upper bar has been turned into a bent stroke with a hook rising upwards at the left end. In the second *ja* (Col. III, b) the lower bar has been dropped in order to keep the foot of the sign free. The Pehlevi letter probably is an analogous development. The *Zain* of the Papyri (Col. II) is

[1] Edict III, 9 in *raja,* IV, 16 in *raja,* V, 19 in *raja,* V, 24 in *praja,* VIII, 35 in *raja,* XII, 1 in *raja.*

again [55] much more advanced and unfit to be considered the original of the Kharoṣṭhī sign.

No 8. With respect to the representative of the *Cheth* I differ from all my predecessors. The Aramaic letter, such as it is found in the Saqqārah inscription (Col. I, a—c), in Teima and various other documents[1] is exactly the same as the Kharoṣṭhī palatal sibilant *śa*. The pronunciation of the Indian *śa* comes very close to the German *ch* in *ich*, *lich* etc.,[2] and hence the utilisation of the otherwise redundant *Cheth* for the expression of *śa* appears to me perfectly regular and normal.

No 9. The derivation of *ya* (Col. III) from the Aramaic *Yod* has been generally assumed, and it has been noticed that the Kharoṣṭhī sign is identical with the late Palmyrenian and Pehlevi forms (Euting, Cols. 21—25, 30—32, 35—39, 58), which of course are independent analogous developments, as well as that it resembles the *Yod* of the Papyri (Col. II, c and Euting, Cols. 14—17), where however the centre of the letter is mostly filled in with ink. Still closer comes the first sign (Col. II, b) from the Stele Vaticana, and it may be that a form like the latter is the real prototype. But I think the possibility is not precluded, that the Kharoṣṭhī *ya* may be an Indian modification of a form like the more ancient Assyrian Aramaic sign in Col. I, a, which differs only by the retention of the second bar at the right lower end. The rejection of this bar was necessary in accordance with the principles of the Kharoṣṭhī, stated above, and may therefore be put down as an Indian modification. The height of the Kharoṣṭhī *ya* seems to indicate that its prototype had not yet been reduced to the diminutive size, which it usually has in the Papyri, but which is not yet observable in the otherwise differing letters of the Teima and Saqqārah inscriptions.

No 10. The connexion of *ka* (Col. III) with the Aramaic *Kaph* is asserted by M. J. Halévy, but he compares the sign of the Papyri [56] (Col. II), which is very dissimilar. I think, there can be no doubt that the Kharoṣṭhī letter is a modification

---

[1] It occurs even in the Papyri though these offer mostly more advanced, rounded forms.

[2] Prof. A. Kuhn long ago expressed his belief that etymologically *śa* is derived from *ka* through a palatal *χa*.

of the Babylonian *Kaph* in Col. I, b, which was turned round in order to avoid a collision with *la* and further received the little bar at the top for the sake of clearer distinction from *pa*. The sign in Col. I, a, which likewise comes from Babylon, has been added in order to show the development of that in Col. I, b, from the oldest form.

No 11. *Lamed*, consisting of a vertical with an appendage at the foot had, as stated above, to be turned topsy-turvy in order to yield the Kharoṣṭhī *la*, with which Dr. Taylor and M. Halévy have identified it. Moreover, the curve which then stood at the top was converted into a broken line[1] and attached a little below the top of the vertical, in order to avoid a collision with *A*. The signs of the Papyri (Col. II) are mostly far advanced and cursive, so that they can not be considered the prototypes of the Kharoṣṭhī *la*.

No 12. The Kharoṣṭhī *ma* (Col. III, a—c) is, as has been generally recognised, not much more than the head of the Aramaic *Mem* in Col. I. The first two forms, which are common in Aśoka's Edicts and the second of which occurs also on the Indo-Grecian coins, still show remnants of the side-stroke and of the central vertical or slanting stroke. But they have been placed on the left instead of on the right. The mutilation of the letter is no doubt due, as has been suggested by others, to the introduction of the vowel signs, which would have given awkward forms, and the fact of the mutilation is indicated by its size, as it is always much smaller than the other Kharoṣṭhī signs. The curved head appears in the Saqqārah *Mem*, which I have chosen for comparison, as well as on Babylonian Seals and Gems (Euting, Col. 8, e) and in the Carpentras inscription (Euting, Col. 13, c), and the later forms from Palmyra prove that it must have been common. The *Mem* of the Papyri are again much more cursive and unsuited for comparison.

[57] No 13. Regarding *na* (Col. III, a), which is clearly the *Nun* of the Saqqārah (Col. I, a—b) Teima, Assyrian and Babylonian inscriptions, it need be only pointed out that the

---

[1] The *la* of the Edicts almost invariably shows the broken line. The later inscriptions offer instead a curve open below.

forms of the Papyri are also in this case further advanced than those of the Kharoṣṭhī. The *na,* given in Col. III, b, is a peculiar Indian development, rather rare in the Aśoka Edicts.

No 14. The identity of *sa* with the Aramaic *Samech* (Col. I) has hitherto not been recognised. Nevertheless the not uncommon form of *sa* with the polygonal or angular head, given in Col. III, permits us to assert that also in this case the Gandharians used for the notation of their dental sibilant the sign which one would expect to be employed for the purpose. The top stroke and the upper portion of the right side of the Kharoṣṭhī *sa* correspond very closely to the upper hook of the *Samech* of Teima, being only made a little broader. The little slanting bar in the centre of the *Samech* may be identified with the downward stroke, attached to the left of the top line of *sa,* and the lower left side of *sa* appears to be the corresponding portion of the *Samech,* turned round towards the left in order to effect a connexion with the downward stroke. These remarks will become most easily intelligible, if the component parts of the two letters are separated. Then we have for *Samech*  and for *sa* . The forms, in which the right portion of the head of *sa* is rounded, are of course cursive. The Teima form of the *Samech* with the little horn at the left end of the top stroke is unique in the older inscriptions. But the Palmyrenian letters (Euting, Cols. 24—29, 32—33, 37, 39—40), though otherwise considerably modified, prove that the *Samech* with an upward twist must have been common. Finally, the corresponding Nabataean characters (Euting, Cols. 46—47), are almost exactly the same as the Kharoṣṭhī *sa* and show that the changes, assumed above, are easy and have actually been made again in much later times. The signs of the Papyri are again far advanced and unsuited for comparison.

No 15. The identity of *pa* with *Phe* is plain enough (Thomas, Taylor, Halévy). The Semitic letter (Col. I) has been turned round [58] in order to avoid the resemblance to *A.* The form with a hook, attached to the right top of the vertical (Col. III, a) occurs still a few times in the Mansehra version of the Edicts. Usually the hook or curve is placed lower, as in Col. III, b, and it may be noted that in the Mansehra *pa* it is attached nearly always very high up, in the Shāhbāzgarhī letter not rarely lower.

No 16. On phonetic grounds it may, of course, be expected that *Tsade* should have been used for the Indian *ca*. But the recognition of the real Kharoṣṭhī representative has been impeded by the circumstance that the earlier tables of the alphabet neglect to give the form of *ca*, which comes closest to the Semitic letter, viz. that with the angular head (Col. III). The tables give only the *ca* with the semicircular top, though the other form is by no means rare in the Edicts and is used also in the *cha* (Col. IV) of the same documents and even survives in the late Kharoṣṭhī inscriptions of the first and second centuries of our era. If the angular *ca* is chosen for comparison, it is not difficult to explain how the Kharoṣṭhī sign was developed. The Hindus made the top of the *Tsade* (Col. I, a—b) by itself, separating it from the remainder of the vertical, and omitted in accordance with the principles of their writing, which do not admit more than two strokes at the tops of letters (see above p. 52) the small hook on the right of the angle. Next, they placed the lower part of the vertical under the point of the angle and in doing so added a small flourish to the top of this line, which in course of time became an important element of their sign. The *Tsades* of the Papyri (Col. II) come very close to the Kharoṣṭhī *ca* and the second even shows the small projection on the left, just below the top. Nevertheless they are only independent analogous developments. For in both, the long line on the left has been made continuous with one stroke of the pen and the hook or curve on the right has been added afterwards. Moreover, in the sign of Col. II, b, it is very plain that the small projection on the left of the main line, which makes the letter so very like the Kharoṣṭhī *ca*, has been caused by a careless continuation of the right hand hook across the vertical.

[59] No 17. The utilisation of the ancient *Qoph* for the expression of *kha* in the Brāhma alphabet suggests the conjecture that the curious Kharoṣṭhī sign for *kha* may be derived from the corresponding Aramaic character. And in the Serapeum inscription the *Qoph* (Col. I) has a form which comes very close to the Kharoṣṭhī *kha*. Only the upward stroke on the

left is shorter and there is still a small remnant of the original central line of the ancient North-Semitic character. The smaller Teima inscription[1] (Euting, Col. 10) has a *Qoph,* in which the central pendant has been attached to the lower end of the curve (compare above the case of the Kharoṣṭhī *ha*). These two forms, it seems to me, furnish sufficient grounds, for the assumption, that in the earlier Aramaic writing the component parts of the looped *Qoph* (Col. II, c) were disconnected and arranged in a manner, which might lead to the still simpler Kharoṣṭhī sign, where the central pendant seems to have been added to the upstroke on the left in order to gain room for the vowel-signs. To this conclusion points also the first corresponding sign of the Saqqārah inscription (Euting, Col. 11, a) though the top has been less fully developed and the ancient central pendant has been preserved much better.[2]

No 18. *Ra* (Col. III) has been recognised as the representative of *Resh* by all previous writers. But it deserves to be noted that the sign, which comes nearest to the Kharoṣṭhī letter is the character from Saqqārah, given in Col. I, b.[3] The Papyri offer mostly more advanced forms with top lines sloping downwards towards the right.

No 19. Regarding *Shin* (Col. I) and its Kharoṣṭhī counterpart, the sign for the lingual sibilant *ṣa* (Col. III), see above p. 100. I may add that round forms of *Shin* appear already on the Babylonian Seals and Gems (Euting, Col. 8).

No 20. The oldest representatives of the Semitic *Taw* appear in the dental *tha* (Col. IV, a), which consists of the old Assyrian [60] Aramaic *Taw* (Col. I, a) of the 8th century B. C.,[4] or of a slight modification of the very similar Saqqārah letter (Col. I, b) (turned round from the right to the left) *plus* the bar of aspiration on the right, about which more will be said below, and in the lingual *ṭa* (Col. IV, b—c), where the second stroke on the right in *b* and on the left in *c* denotes the organic difference or, as the Hindus would say, the differ-

[1] Compare the end of l. 1 of the facsimile in M. Ph. Berger's *Histoire de l'Écriture,* p. 217.

[2] Compare also the sign from the Lion of Abydos, Euting, Col. 7.

[3] Compare also Euting, Col. 7, b.

[4] Ante p. 72.

ence in the Varga. In the second form of *ṭa* (Col. IV, c) the bar, which originally stood at the side, has been added at the top, and out of such a form the dental *ta* (Col. III) appears to have been developed. Its top line has been lengthened considerably and the downstroke has been shortened and bent in order to avoid a collision with *va* and *ra*. The steps, which led to its formation, are therefore (1)  or , (2) 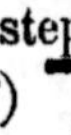, (3) 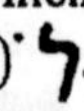.

With respect to the Derivative Signs, my views are as follows.

(1) The aspiration is expressed by a curve, by a hook or by a straight stroke, which latter, as the case of *bha* (No 2, Col. IV, a—b) shows, is a cursive substitute for the curve. At the same time the original form of the unaspirated letters is sometimes slightly modified. The curve appears on the right of the *ga* in *gha* (No 3, Col. IV) at the top of *da* in *dha* (No 4, Col. IV, a) without any change in the original forms. In *bha* (No 2, Col. IV, a) it is attached to the right of *ba*, the wavy top of which is converted into a simple straight stroke, from the middle of which the vertical line hangs down. The same sign shows also frequently in the Aśoka Edicts a hook for the curve and as frequently a cursive straight stroke (No 2, Col. IV, b), slanting downwards towards the right. The hook alone is found in *ṭha* (No 20, Col. IV, d),[1] which has been derived from the preceding form of *ṭa* (No 20, Col. IV, c) by the addition of a hook opening upwards. The straight stroke alone is found, on the left of the original letter and slanting downwards, in *jha* (No 7, Col. IV), and likewise on the left but rising upwards,[2] in *pha* (No 15, Col. IV). In *tha* (No 20, Col. IV, a) [61] the stroke of aspiration appears on the right. It has the same position in *chha* (No 16, Col. IV) and in *ḍha* (No 4, Col. IV, c). But in the former sign the small slanting stroke at the top of the vertical on the left has been straightened and combined with the sign of aspiration into a bar across the vertical. In *ḍha* the whole head of the unaspirated letter (No 4, Col. IV, b) has been flattened down and reduced to a single stroke, which together with the sign of aspiration forms the bar across the top of the vertical.

---

[1] The sign in the table is really *ṭho*.

[2] There are also examples, in which the stroke is made straight.

With respect to the origin of the mark of aspiration I can only agree with Dr. Taylor, who explains it as a cursive form of *ha*, *The Alphabet*, vol. II, p. 260, note 1. The manner, in which it was attached in each particular case, seems to have been regulated merely by considerations of convenience and the desire to produce easily distinguishable signs. The way in which the hook or curve of aspiration has been used in the Brāhma alphabet is analogous. There too, it is added very irregularly sometimes to the top, sometimes to the middle and more frequently to the foot of the letters, where properly it ought to stand.[1] If the Kharoṣṭhī characters never show it at the foot, the cause is no doubt the desire to keep the lower ends of the signs free from encumbrances, as has been noticed above p. 100.

The device for expressing the lingualisation in *ṭa* (No 20, Col. IV, b—c) and *ṇa* (No 13, Col. IV, a) is very similar to that sometimes used in the Brāhma alphabet, in order to indicate the change of the Varga or class of the letter. A straight stroke, added originally on the right, serves this purpose in the Bhaṭṭiprolu *ḷa*, in the Brāhma *ṇa*, *ña* and *ṅa*.[2] The case of the Kharoṣṭhī *ṭa* has been stated above in the remarks on the representatives of *Taw*. With respect to *ṇa* it is sufficient to point out that it has been developed from the *na* No 13, Col. III, b, by a slight prolongation of the right hand stroke. The case of the lingual *ḍa* (No 4, Col. IV, b) is doubtful. Possibly it may be derived from an older dental *da*, like that [62] in No 4, Col. I, a, by the addition of a short vertical straight line on the right, which coalesced with the vertical of the *da* and thus formed the sign with the open square at the head. But it is also possible that the Aramaic alphabet, imported into India, possessed several variants for *Daleth*, and that the heavier one (No 4, Col. I, b) was chosen by the Hindus to express the heavier lingual *ḍa*, while the lighter or more cursive one was utilised for the dental *da*.

The origin of the remaining two Kharoṣṭhī consonantic signs, the palatal *ña* (No 13, Col. IV, b, c) and of the Anusvāra in *maṃ* (No 12, Col. IV) has been already settled by Mr. E.

---

[1] Ante p. 76f.

[2] Ante p. 76.

Thomas. He has recognised that the palatal *ña* consists of two dental *na*, joined together, and it may be added that in the Aśoka Edicts sometimes the right half and sometimes the left half is only rudimentary, as shown by the two specimens given in the Table. He has also asserted that the Anusvāra is nothing but a subscript small *ma*, which proposition is perfectly evident in the form given in the table, less apparent, but not less true in other cases, for which I must refer to Tafel I. 29. IV of my *Grundriss der indischen Palaeographie.*

As regards, finally, the Kharoṣṭhī vowel system, and the compound consonants (not given in the accompanying table) I can only agree with Mr. E. Thomas, Professor A. Weber and Sir A. Cunningham, that they have been elaborated with the help of the Brāhma alphabet. Among the vowel signs the medial ones have been framed first and afterwards only the initial *I, U, E, O* (No 1, Col. IV, a—d). They consist merely of straight strokes, which (1) in the case of *i* go across the left side of the upper or uppermost lines of the consonant, (2) in the case of *u* slant away from the left side of the foot, (3) in the case of *e* stand, slanting from the right to the left, on the top line of the consonant (mostly on the left side) and (4) in the case of *o* stand below the top line (compare *ṭho,* No 20, Col. IV, d) or slant away from the upper half of the vertical as in *O.* The position of the four medial vowels thus closely agrees with that of the corresponding signs of the Brāhma alphabet, where *i, e* and *o* stand at the top of the consonants and *u* at the foot. This circumstance [63] alone is sufficient to raise the suspicion that there is a direct connexion between the two systems of vowel-notation; see add. p. 124. And the suspicion becomes stronger, if some further facts are taken into consideration. In the Brāhma alphabet of the Aśoka Edicts the medial *e* and *u* are mostly expressed by straight strokes. The medial *o,* too, consists at least in one case, Delhi Sivalik Pillar Edict, VII. 2, l. 2 *(nigohāni)* of a straight bar across the top of the consonant, and has the same form frequently, on the Persian *sigloi* (see below p. 113) and in the Bhaṭṭiprolu inscriptions. Again the medial *i* of the Girnār version is expressed by a shallow curve, which in many instances is not distinguishable from the medial *ā.* Thus even the oldest Brāhma documents furnish instances, in which all the four vowels, expressed in the Kharoṣṭhī by straight strokes, have exactly the same form, and it is very probable that in the ordinary writing of every day life these cursive forms were in the case of *o* and *i* much more frequent than the Edicts show, as well as that they go back to earlier times than the third century B. C. If, finally, the fact is added, that the Kharoṣṭhī, like the Brāhmī considers the short *a* to be inherent in all consonants and does not express it by any sign, it becomes difficult to avoid the inference, drawn already by Professor Weber, that the Kharoṣṭhī system of medial vowels has been borrowed from the older alphabet.

The marking of the initial *I, U, E, O* (No 1, Col. IV, a—d) by *A plus* the corresponding medial vowel-sign is, of course, an independent invention of the framer or framers of the Kharoṣṭhī and probably due to a desire to simplify the more cumbersome system of the Brāhmī, which first developed the initial vowels, next used them in combination with the consonants and finally reduced their shapes in such combinations to simple strokes and curves.[1] Similar attempts have been repeatedly made on Indian ground. The modern Devanāgarī has its ओ and औ since the thirteenth or fourteenth century, the modern Gujarātī has its *E, AI, O* and *AU*, consisting of *A plus* the medial vowel-signs, and [64] the Tibetan alphabet, framed out of the *Vartu* letters of the seventh century A. D., expresses even I and *U* by A *plus* *i* and *u*. These examples show that the idea at all events came naturally to the Hindus and that it is unnecessary to look for a foreign source of its origin.

The rules for the treatment of the compound consonants again agree so fully with those of the Brāhmī, especially with those adopted in the Girnār version, that they can only be considered as copies of the latter.

(1) Double consonants like *kka, tta,* and groups of unaspirated consonants like *kkha, ttha* etc., are expressed by the second element alone, except in the case of two nasals of the same class, where the first may be optionally expressed by the Anusvāra as in *aṃña* or *aña*. Three times, however, a double

---

[1] Ante p. 77 ff.

ma is used in the word *samma°* *(samyak-pratipatti)*, Shāhbāzgarhī Ed. IX. 19, XI. 23 and XIII. 5.[1]

(2) Groups of dissimilar consonants are expressed by ligatures of the signs, except if the first is a nasal, for which the Anusvāra is used throughout.

(3) In the ligatures the sign for the consonants, to be pronounced first, stands above and the next is interlaced with the lower end of the first, except in the case of groups with *ra*, where *ra* is almost invariably placed below.[2] The forms of the Kharoṣṭhī ligatures are shaped exactly like those of the Brāhmī and, like these, illustrations of the grammatical term *saṃyuktākṣara* "a conjunct syllable". The neglect of non-aspirates, preceding aspirates, and of the double consonants, with the exception of the nasals, which can be marked without trouble by the Anusvāra, is, as already pointed out, a clerks' trick and the same as that used in the Brāhmī lipi[3] of the Prakrit inscriptions. The treatment of *ra* in groups is closely analogous to that adopted in Girnār, where this letter or its cursive representative always occupies the same position, whether it must be pronounced before or after the consonant with which it is combined. There is, however, this [65] difference that in the Girnār Brāhmī *ra* stand always at the top and in the Kharoṣṭhī invariably at the foot. The one writes *e. g.* *rta* for *rta* and *tra,* and the other *tra* both for *rta* and *tra.*

These remarks at all events suffice to show that a rational derivation of the Kharoṣṭhī from the Aramaic of the Akhaemenian Period, based on fixed principles, is perfectly possible and the attempt has this advantage that it shows some letters, as *da, ka* and *ta,* to be closely connected with Mesopotamian forms, which *a priori* might be expected to have been used by the writers of the Satraps, ruling over the extreme east of the Persian empire. If the ruins of the eastern Persian provinces are ever scientifically explored and ancient Aramaic inscrip-

---

[1] In the third case Sir A. Cunningham's copy of the Shāhbāzgarhī Edicts in the Corpus Inscr. Ind., vol. I, Pl. II, gives the *mma* correctly.

[2] There is only one exception in the Mansehra version Ed. V, 24, *karṭabhikare.*

[3] Compare also the Grundriss, I, 11, § 14.

tions are found there, forms much closer to the Kharoṣṭhī will no doubt turn up.

The third and last point, the existence of which has been indicated above, furnishes perhaps the most convincing proof for Dr. Taylor's theory. It is simply this, that Mr. E. J. Rapson has discovered of late on Persian silver *sigloi*, coming from the Panjab, both Kharoṣṭhī and Brāhma letters. Mr. Rapson was good enough to show me specimens, belonging to the British Museum, during my late visit to England, and I can vouch for the correctness of his observation. I think, I can do not better than quote his paragraph on the Persian coins in India from the MS. of his contribution to Mr. Trübner's *Grundriss der Indo-Arischen Philologie und Altertumskunde*, which will appear in Vol. II, Section 3 B:—

§ 7. "During the period of the Achaemenid rule (c. 510—331 B. C.) Persian coins circulated in the Panjāb. Gold double *staters* were actually struck in India, probably in the latter half of the 4th cent. B. C. [Babelon, *Les Perses Achéménides*, pp. IX, XX, 16, Pl. II, 16—19; 27]. Many of the silver *sigloi*, moreover, bear countermarks so similar to the native punch marks[1] as to make it seem probable that the two classes of coins were in circulation together; and this probability is increased by the occurrence on *sigloi*, recently acquired by the British Museum, of Brāhma and Kharoṣṭhī letters."[2]

[66] This appears to me sufficient to establish the conclusion that the Kharoṣṭhī did exist in India during the Akhaemenian times and did not originate after the fall of the empire. At the same time we learn that before 331 B. C. the Kharoṣṭhī and the Brāhma letters were used together in the Panjab, just as was the case in the 3rd and 2nd centuries B. C.

In conclusion I may offer a suggestion regarding the name of the script of Gandhāra. The Buddhist tradition derives the term Kharoṣṭhī from the name of its inventor who is said to have been called *Kharoṣṭha* "Ass'-lip". I am ready to accept this as true and historical, because the ancient Hindus have

[1] Babelon, *op. cit.*, p. XI attributes these countermarks to other provinces of Asia.

[2] Compare now his article in the Journal Royal Asiatic Society 1895, p. 865 ff.

very curious names—apparently nicknames.[1] Thus we find already in the Vedas three men, called *Śunaḥśepa, Śunaḥpuccha* and *Śunolāṅgūla* "Dog's-tail", and *Śunaka* "Little-Dog" is the progenitor of a very numerous race. Again a *Kharījaṅgha* "She-Ass'-Leg" is according to a Gaṇa in Pāṇini's Grammar likewise the father of a tribe or family.

---

[1] But compare now the interesting article of Professor A. Ludwig in the Gurupūjākaumudī p. 68. Professor A. Ludwig takes *kharoṭṭha* to be the original form of the name and *kharoṣṭha* a false transliteration into Sanskrit. And he considers *kharoṭṭha* to be the Indian representative of a possible, though not actually found, Aramaic ḫarūtthā חרותתא "engraving, writing". In favour of Professor A. Ludwig's view that *kharoṣṭha* may be due to the false transliteration of a foreign word it may urged that its derivative *kharoṣṭhī*, more usually spelt *kharoṣṭī* and even *kharosti* or *kharostrī* (Mahāvastu p. 135, l. 5), occurs only in Northern Buddhist texts and that these are full of similar blunders in the conversion of Pali words into Sanskrit. If the actual and frequent occurrence of *ḫarūtthā* should be proved hereafter, I should be quite ready to give up my conjecture in favour of his. Regarding other derivations of the name Kharoṣṭha see, A. Weber, Indische Streifen, vol. III, p. 8 f.

Appendix II.

The Origin of the ancient Brāhma Numerals.

In my *Grundriss der Indischen Paläographie*, p. 77f., I have briefly discussed the various theories regarding the origin of the ancient system of numeral notation found in the older inscriptions and MSS. which are written in Brahma characters. And I have expressed the opinion that in spite of serious difficulties Dr. Burnell's suggestion, according to which it has been derived from an Egyptian source, seems for the present more probable than any of the other attempts at an explanation of its origin. As Dr. Burnell's remarks on this point in his Elements of South Indian Palaeography, p. 65f., are only general and very brief, a more detailed comparison of the two Egyptian systems which can come into question, the hieratic and its immediate derivative, the demotic, will not be superfluous. In order to facilitate it the accompanying Plate III[1] exhibits in Col. I the most important forms of the hieratic numerals according to Professor Euting's table, given under No LXXIV in the Palaeographic Society's Oriental Series, in Col. II the demotic signs according to the plates, appended to Professor Brugsch's Demotische Grammatik, and in Cols III—IV the Indian numerals according to the originals from which Cols I—IV of Tafel IX of my Grundriss have been compiled. Among the figures for 6, Col. III, c, shows however an additional sign, that of the Sahasrām Edict, which has been omitted in the Grundriss.

The resemblance of the principles of the Egyptian and Indian systems is, if not complete, at least very great. Both

---

[1] Drawn by Mr. Böhm and etched by Messrs Angerer and Göschl of Vienna.

have separate signs for 1—9, 10—90, 100 and 1000. In both the numerals 1—3 are expressed by strokes, either vertical or horizontal[1] or by combinations thereof and the symbols begin with 4. In both the signs for 200 and 300 consist of that for 100, united respectively with the signs for one and two.[2] The not very important differences are (1) that the Indians form 2000 and 3000 on the same principle as 200 and 300, while the Egyptians add in these cases the signs for two and three to the symbol for 1000; (2) that the Indians form 400—900 and 4000—9000 by the combinations of 100 with 4—9 and of 1000 with 4—9, while the Egyptians have at least for 400 the combination 100 + 3; (3) and that the Egyptians have a separate sign for 10,000 which is wanting in the Indian system. The first two discrepancies may possibly be due to the formalism of the Hindus, which may have induced them to reject the vacillation in the Egyptian system and to rigorously adhere to one and the same principle.

If we turn to the comparison of the several symbols beginning with 4, it is evident that the oldest Indian forms of eight out of the total of seventeen come close to the hieratic or to both the hieratic and the demotic. It is also evident that those differences, which are observable, are due either to the desire to simplify the cumbersome Egyptian signs or to the tendency to transform them into Brāhma letters and syllables.[3] The five of Col. V, a, appears to be derived from the hieratic sign of Col. I, which has been turned from the left to the right, while the side-limb has been attached lower in order to obtain an approach to the Brāhma *tra*. The six of Col. III, a, likewise comes close to that of Col. I, the slight alteration being made in order to obtain the looped Brāhma *ja*, from which latter the signs in Col. III, b—c, and in Col. V, a looped *sa* and *phra* or *phu*, seem to have been developed in their turn. The seven of Cols IV—V looks like

---

[1] Horizontal strokes occur in the Egyptian signs for 2 and 3, referring to the days of the month.

[2] The strokes no doubt represent an original repetition of the symbols for 100, and it is as if the Romans wrote CI and CII for CC and CCC.

[3] Regarding this tendency and its ultimate effects, see the Grundriss, p. 75 ff.

a modification of that in Col. I, a, made in order to obtain a sign similar to *gra* or *gu*, the later Indian letter-symbol. The nine of Cols IV—V agrees almost exactly with the hieratic and demotic signs in Cols I—II. The fifty of Col. III, b, is produced by a slight simplification of the symbols in Cols I—II, while the fifty of Col. III, a, has been turned round from the left to the right. More strongly modified and more remote from the hieratic signs are the Indian symbols for 60 and 70 in Col. V, the second of which has been converted into a Brāhma *pū*. Finally the thousand of Cols IV—V, especially the second, look like derivatives from the corresponding Egyptian signs in Cols I—II, which however have been turned topsy-turvy and slightly altered in order to produce the Brāhma syllables *ro, cu* and *dhu*.

The list of closely similar signs will also include the hundred, if it may be assumed that the Indian signs of Col. V, which look like modifications of the hieratic in Col. I, in reality are older than those of the Aśoka Edicts and of the Nānāghāt inscription in Cols III—IV. And it seems to me possible to defend such an assumption. For the Andhra and Kṣatrapa signs for 100, which are also found very frequently in the Sanskrit inscriptions of the 5th—8th cent. A. D. from Western India as well as in the Kaliṅga landgrants of the 8th cent., in all probability represent the syllable *śu*.[1] Its *śa* has a form which corresponds to the oldest Semitic *Shin*[2] with two angles but has been turned topsy-turvy, and which is older than the *śa* of the third century B. C.[3] Further, with the assumption that the hundred of Col. V is really the oldest, it becomes possible to explain the origin of those in Col. III—IV. As the Aśoka sign opposite 200[4] in Col. III, a, clearly shows, they represent the Brāhma syllable *su*, and *su* is in Prakrit the regular represen-

---

[1] See the Grundriss, p. 77 and note 20, where two inscriptions are referred to, in which more modern forms of *śu* or *śa* appear in the hundred.

[2] See above Plate I, 21, Cols I—II.

[3] See above Plate I, 21, Col. V, as well as Tafel II, 37, I—II, XI etc. of the Grundriss, and compare the remark made above p. 71.

[4] Equivalent to the ordinary *su* with an unusual elongation of the vertical, which seems to do duty for the additional horizontal stroke, commonly found in 200 on the right side.

tative of a Sanskrit *śu.* The process of the development of the Indian hundreds would therefore be as follows. The Hindus first converted the hieratic hundred into an archaic *śu* (Col. V). Next they substituted its phonetic Prakrit representative *su* for it (200, Col. III, a) and finally they again modified the form of *su* in order to indicate that it has not a phonetic but a numeral value (200, Col. III, b—c; 100—700, Col. IV).

With the admission of another conjecture the cases of close resemblance will extend to a tenth sign. It is undeniable that the Indian sign for 40 in Col. V is almost exactly identical with the Egyptian symbols for 30 in Cols I—II. As the Indian 30 shows a remote similarity to the Egyptian 40, it is tempting to assume that the Hindus made the signs for 30 and 40 exchange their places, be it through negligence or for some other reason.

The remaining signs differ much more. But it is quite imaginable that the four and eight of Col. I may have be converted respectively into the *ka* of Col. III[1] and the *hra* or *hu* of Col. V, that the ten of Col. I, being turned from the left to the right, became the *ṭhū* of Cols IV—V, and that the twenty of Col. I by a considerable simplification yielded the *tha* of Col. V.[2] The most difficult signs are, as Dr. Burnell has also recognised, those for 80 and 90. There is no actual resemblance between the Egyptian and the Indian forms. But it deserves to be noted that in both the hieratic and the Indian systems they apparently form a separate group, in which the higher numeral is differentiated from the lower one by the addition of a second line, standing in the hieratic sign below and running in the Indian ninety horizontally across the middle.

---

[1] The four of Col. V. (compare also those of 400 and 4000 in Col. IV), which may be read *kī* and *pka*, are in my opinion later developments from the simple *ka.* The apparent vowel or *pa*-mark at the top is probably merely formed out of a flourish, which originally indicated that the letter had not a phonetic value; compare the late *ṅka, ṅkā* in Tafel IX, Col. XXIV—XXV of the Grundriss, where a similar striving at differentiation is perceptible, and the remarks in the Grundriss, I, 11, p. 75.

[2] On the supposition that this is the older form, the *ṭha* of Col. IV in 20,000 might be regarded as a phonetic substitute.

The results of this comparison, the nearly complete identity of the principles of the two systems and the closer or remoter resemblances between the great majority of their symbols, raise, it seems to me, a strong presumption in favour of Dr. Burnell's theory, which, however, has to be modified by the admission that the hieratic signs rather than the demotic are the parents of the Indian Brāhma numerals and that the tendency to frame out of them Brāhma letters or syllables and again to differentiate these from the ordinary letters is already visible in a number of cases. And I believe that this tendency is due to the fact that the Hindus since ancient times were accustomed to express numerals by such words as *rūpa* = 1, *bhūta* = 5 and so forth.[1] In order to convert Dr. Burnell's theory into an absolute certainty, the discovery of more ancient signs of the third and earlier centuries B. C. is required as well as the discovery of historical or traditional information regarding an ancient intercourse between India and Egypt. For the present this is entirely wanting and the only way, in which one could try to account for the introduction of the Egyptian numerals into India, would be to conjecture that the early Indian navigators and merchants might have reached countries which stood under Egyptian influence or might have met on their voyages with Egyptian traders. But such a conjecture is, of course, precarious, as long as it is not supported by collateral proof.

---

[1] See the Grundriss, I, 11, p. 80ff.

Addenda.

P. 9, l. 28. Another case of a letter of defiance *(paṇṇa)* sent to a king by his adversaries is mentioned in Jātaka, No. 23, Fausböll, vol. I, p. 178 (Rhys Davids).

P. 10, l. 12. Promissory notes *(paṇṇa)* and their redemption by payment are mentioned in the introduction to Jātaka No 40, Fausböll, vol. I, p. 227, l. 3 f., and p. 230, l. 1 ff. (Rhys Davids).

P. 11, l. 14. According to Jātaka No 388 (Fausböll, vol. III, p. 292) the future Buddha caused the judicial rules to be written in a book *(potthaka)* and recommended that, in future, cases should be decided, after reference to it. A book *(potthaka)* is mentioned also in the Uddālaka Jātaka No 487, Fausböll, vol. IV, p. 487, l. 17 f, where Uddālaka's preparations, intended to captivate the king, are described as follows: "But he himself took with him eight or ten disputant Pandits, placed a lovely book *(potthaka)* on a charming reading desk *(ādhāraka)* and sat down, surrounded by his pupils, on a prepared seat which was furnished with a support for the back". Here the book can only be a MS. of a literary work, and the reading desk is probably one of those little tripods, consisting of three laquered pieces of wood, which are commonly used by the Jaina Yatis at their *vācanās*. The whole description is merely an accessory without any importance for the story and may be an interpolation, as its rather modern look suggests.

P. 31, l. 5. From Mr. Halhed's Grammar of the Bengal language, p. 17 ff. (Calcutta, 1778), to which Dr. B. Liebich has drawn my attention, it appears that about the end of the last century the Bengal schoolmasters still used a set of twelve tables, including chiefly compound letters, which may be remotely connected with Hiuen Tsiang's twelve *chang* and Huilin's twelve *fan*. Mr. Halhed calls them the twelve *Phola,* which name according to the Jonesian transliteration would be *Phalā* and corresponds to the Sanskrit *phalaka,* 'board, tablet', and he states that they severally are *kya, kra, kna, kla, kva, kma, kṛ, kḷ, rka, ṅka, ska* and *siddhi*. He adds that *siddhi* is an abbreviation of *siddhir astu*[1] and that this *Phalā* consists of the sixteen vowels. Mr. Halhed also gives the contents of two other *Phalās* in full, which I copy here in transcription, as his grammar is rather rare.

The Phalā *ṅka* includes:

ṅka	*ṅkha*	*ṅga*	*ṅgha*	*ṅṅa*
ñca	*ñcha*	*ñja*	*ñjha*	*ññα*
ṇṭa	*ṇṭha*	*ṇḍa*	*ṇḍha*	*ṇṇa*
nta	*ntha*	*nda*	*ndha*	*nna*
mpa	*mpha*	*mba*	*mbha*	*mma*
ṅya	*ra*	*ṅla*	*ṅva*	—
ṅśa	*ṅṣa*	*ṅsa*	*ṅha*	*ṅkṣa*, or 34 signs,

and Phalā *ska:*

ska	*skha*	*dga*	*dgha*	*ṅtra*
śca	*ścha*	*bja*	*bjha*	*jña*
ṣṭa	*ṣṭha*	*bḍa*	*bḍha*	*hṇa*
sta	*stha*	*bda*	*bdha*	*hna*
spa	*spha*	*dba*	*dbha*	*hma*
hya	*ra*	*hla*	*hva*	—
ṭśa	*ṭṣa*	*ṭsa*	*ṭha*	*ṭkṣa*,

or again 34 signs.

Though it is evident that the twelve *Phalā* are not identical with Hiulin's twelve *fan,* Mr. Halhed's statements show at all events that a syllabary in twelve sections was actually used in India, at least in Bengal. Probably the division is an old one and has been taken over from one compilation into the other, though the tables underwent changes in other respects.

---

[1] This is a common Maṅgala in Sanskrit books and inscriptions, and stated by Itsing (A Record of the Buddhist Religion, p. 170, Takakusu) to be a name of the whole Indian syllabary. An other work quoted by Mr. Takakusu, (op. cit. p. 171 note) the Siddhakosha of A. D. 880, gives *Siddhām* (sic) as the name of the sixteen vowels.

Full certainty on the exact character of the Indian syllabaries and their history can only be obtained by an examination of the various works, called *lipiviveka*, *mātṛkāviveka*, *varṇamāla* and so forth, mentioned in the publications, connected with the Search for Sanskrit MSS., and in the Catalogues of European libraries. The kindness of Dr. Grierson, who made enquiries regarding the actual occurrence of Huilin's twelve tables through Mr. Prothero, Educational Inspector of Patna, enables to add, that the indigenous schools of Bengal proper still teach the compound letters, but do not teach the combinations of the vowels with the ligatures. But it appears that this is not the case in Bihār, where only the common cursive Kāethī *(Kāyastha-lipi)* is taught. There, as one of the Deputy Inspectors, Mr. Somnāth Jharkhundi says, the instruction in the *varṇamālā* stops, when the boys have mastered the vowels A, Ā . . . Aḥ, the consonants *ka, kha . . . ha*, and the *Bartanī kā, kā . . . kau, kaṃ, kaḥ* and so forth, which latter corresponds exactly to the *Bārākhaḍī* of Western India. Further enquiries in Gujarāt have only had a negative result and have elicited the answer that no tables for compound consonants are known.

Regarding another more extensive syllabary in 18 tables, see Itsing, op. cit., p. LX ff. and p. 170 ff. (Takakusu).

P. 32, l. 6. Read a round-topped *ga* on No 14 instead of on No 13.

P. 38, l. 16. For plate V, No 2 read plate X, No 2.

P. 91, l. 13. The kindness of Dr. S. von Oldenburg has put me in possession of a photograph of a portion of the Kharoṣṭhī MS. brought by M. Petroffski from Khotan, and he has generously given me permission to say here a few words about it. The photograph contains a part of a new version of the brāmhaṇavagga of the Dhammapada in a dialect of Northwestern India, in many respects closely connected with that of the Shāhbāzgarhī rock edicts of Aśoka, but in some respects more advanced in the direction of the later Prakrits. With the Aśoka Edicts the language of the MS. shares the clear distinction between the three Sanskrit sibilants, the preservation of *ra* in groups, the substitution of *o* for final *aṃ* and various characteristic forms like *bramaṇa (brammaṇa)* for *brāhmaṇa* or *brāmhaṇa*. Advanced forms are *e. g. nihaï (nihāï)* for *nidhāya*, *daṇa* (*daṇṇa*) for *daṇḍa*, *china* (*chinna*) for *chinda*, with which latter Pali forms like *puṇṇarīka* for *puṇḍarīka* may be compared.

The principles of its spelling in no way differ from those of the epigraphic Kharoṣṭhī. The long vowels are not marked, the Anusvāra does duty for all nasals in compound consonants, single non-aspirate consonants stand for double ones, and before aspirates the corresponding non-aspirate is left aut. The Buddhists of the Northwest, therefore, found it unnecessary to have recourse to the more accurate spelling of the Pandits, which their brethren in the South have adopted.

The characters show the higly cursive type of the Kuṣana period and come very close to those on the Wardak vase, incised during the reign of Huviṣka. Tho wavy linos in the side-limbs of *ka*, *pa* and *bha* are however more fully developed. On the other hand some very cursive forms of *ka* and *bha*, in which the side-limbs of these letters are attached to the top-lines are wanting in the thirty lines accessible to me. The Pādas of the Ślokas carefully divided and at the end of each Śloka, which almost invariably fills a linc, stands a mark resembling the circular Indian nought, the first sign of interpunctuation found in a Kharoṣṭhī document.

With respect to the exact probable date of the MS., it is difficult to say anything certain, as the question when the famous three Kuṣana kings reigned is not yet settled. If M. S. Lévi (Journ. Asiatique, 1897, p. 1 ff.) is right in contending that even Bazdeo-Vāsudeva belongs to the middle of the first century, the Petroffski MS. cannot be much later than the beginning of our era. But, though I fully agree with M. Lévi in believing that Kaniṣka is *not* the founder of the Śaka era,[1] I do not yet venture to give an unqualified adhesion to his theory, the full proof for which has still to be furnished. For the present I would only say this much that the Petroffski MS. is certainly the oldest Indian MS., yet discovered, and that it perhaps was written in the first century A. D. and certainly

---

[1] See my remarks on this subject and on the reasons why for practical purposes I have adopted the theory of Messrs Fergusson and Oldenberg, in the WZKM. I, 169.

not much later. I believe that, like the Bower MS., it was written in India — as the dialect and the characters suggest, in Gandhāra — and that it was carried by some Buddhist monk into Chinese Turkestan.

P. 110. And it ought to be noted, that while no good reason is apparent why *u* should have been placed at the foot in the Kharoṣṭhī, it is patent that the sprawling  and  of the Brāhmī was not fit to be placed at the top of the consonants, but better suited the position at the foot, where, in letters not ending in verticals, it could be abbreviated, without the risk of confusion with *e*, *ā* and *ai*.

Comparative Table
of
the oldest Semitic and the Brāhma Alphabets.

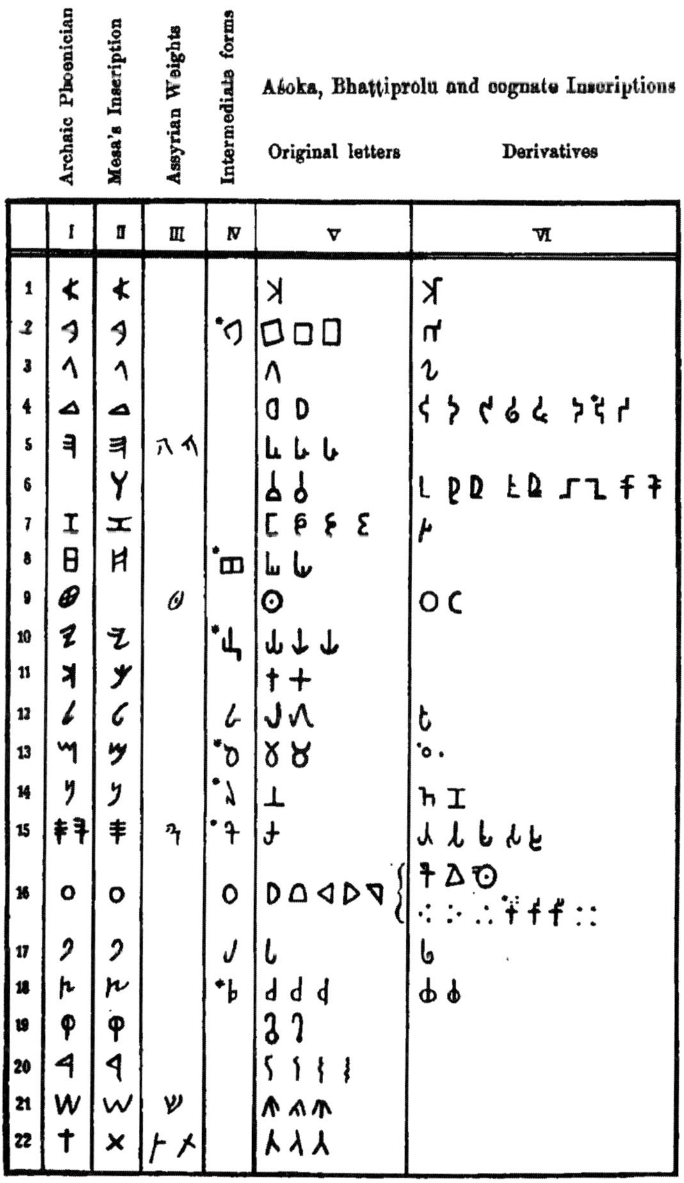

Comparative Table
of
the Perso-Aramaic and the Kharoṣṭhī.

Inscriptions (I) | Papyri (II) | Kharoṣṭhī: Borrowed Letters (III) | Kharoṣṭhī: Derivatives (IV)

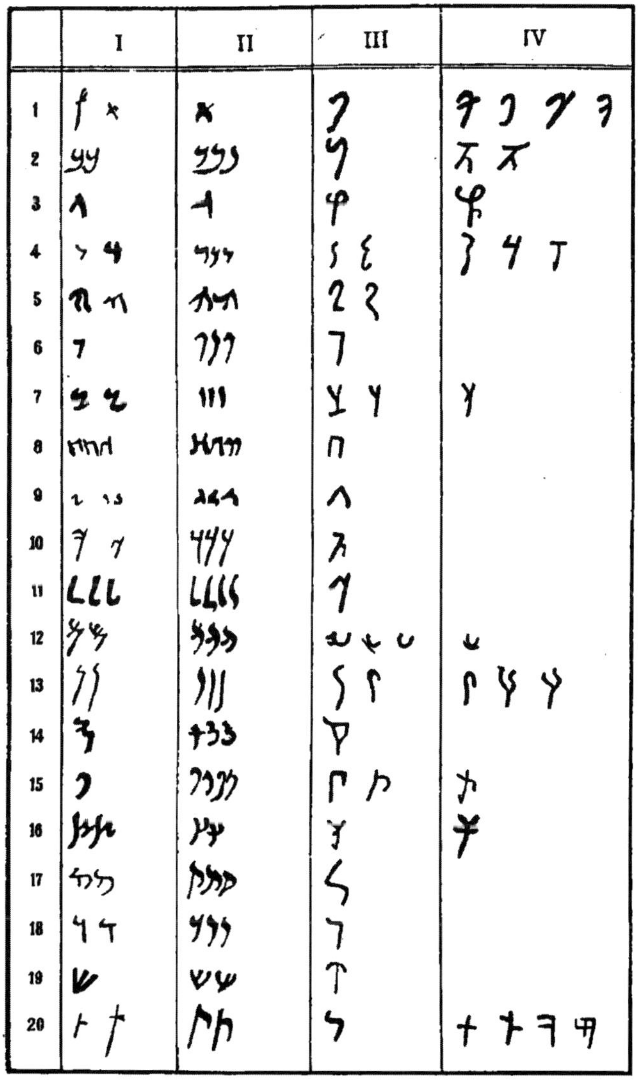

Plate III.

Comparative Table
of
Egyptian Indian Numerals.

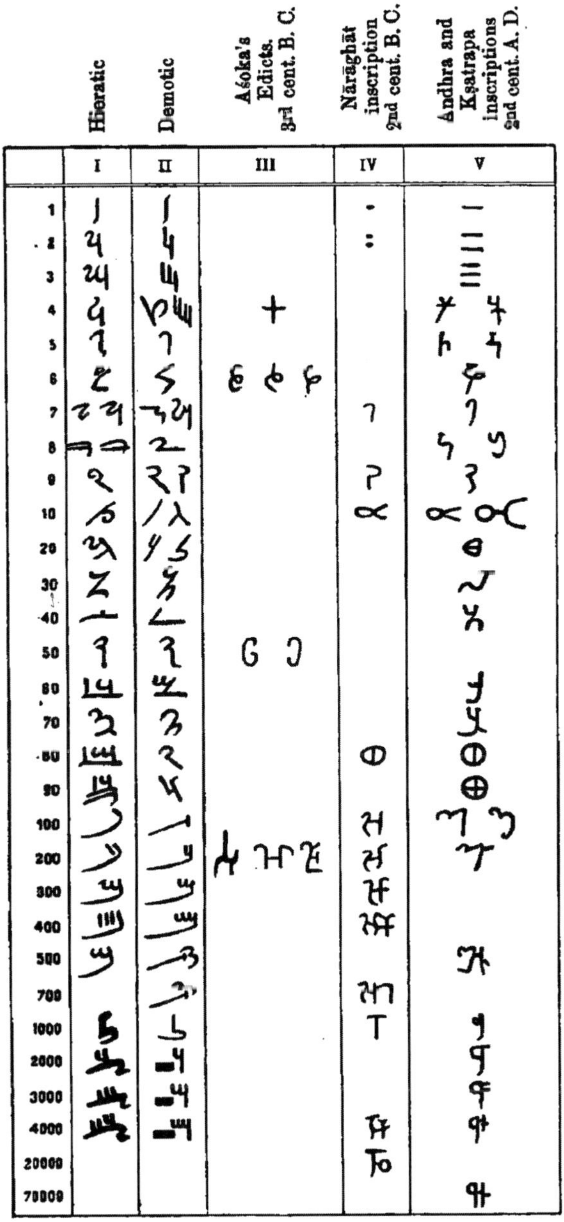